CW00427788

GO HAPPY YOURSELF

STRATEGY, STYLE & SELF-CARE FOR YOUR WORK & BUSINESS SUCCESS

YVONNE PHILLIP

authors
AND CO.

Copyright © 2022 by Yvonne Phillip

ISBN13: Paperback: 979-8-838015-18-1

ISBN: Hardback: 978-1-913728-77-9

All rights reserved.

No part of this book may be reproduced in any form or by any electronic or mechanical means, including information storage and retrieval systems, without written permission from the author, except for the use of brief quotations in a book review.

CONTENTS

PILLAR 3 - SELF-CARE AND MANAGEMENT
GROW AND SUSTAIN FOR CREDIBILITY

DEDICATED TO

My mum, Elena Andrew, for showing me how to be strong, resilient and focused on my dreams. My son, Jonas Andrew-Phillip for giving me my why and something to work for in addition to myself.

INTRODUCTION

Hi there!

So glad you have decided to open the pages of this book to see how it can help you. I'm guessing that you want more happiness, success and visibility in your life, business and / or career. You know what you're good at, that you want to be seen as an expert. Or maybe you are looking to find yourself and create some form of change so you can have a greater sense of achievement and direction.

Whatever your reasons for opening the pages of this book let me reassure you that you are in the right place if:

- You are not sure of who you really are and are fed up with giving to everyone else.
- You feel empty and confused with the direction your life, business or career has taken.
- You need direction in what the next stages of your life may be.
- You are stuck in a funk and feel there's no way out.

- You feel you are always giving to others and have forgotten about yourself.
- You want the clarity to be able to send your message to the wider world.
- You want the confidence to step into who you truly are.
- You want the credibility to shine like the star that you are in person and online.
- You want to attract clients with ease and grow your business.
- You are thinking of a career change or promotion but are not sure what or how.

"Happying" yourself comes from within. Without being visible, without having a holistic brand, you are being overlooked in this busy market that we are all working in. So, what is happiness to you?

- Maybe it's getting a new job or promotion.
- It may be elevating your business and bringing in more clients.
- Is it being seen as an expert and authority within your sector or industry?
- Maybe just the ability to step into your own personal power and be who you want to be.
- Maybe it is having more time with the family.
- Maybe it's having more time for yourself.
- Maybe it's....

The list goes on. Just remember your happiness is determined by you!

Now, in this busy world that we find ourselves in, it takes only a few seconds to create a great first impression. It doesn't matter if this is online or offline, the figures are still the same. You have 3 - 7 seconds before someone forms an opinion of you and 55% of a person's first impression and opinion is made on the visual. It's the way that they see you and the perception they have of you when you walk into a room, they see your pictures, videos, social media and websites etc. If you don't create the right impression within 3 seconds they could be gone, so how do you stand out with expertise and authority? How do you step up with clarity and show up with confidence? This is where 'Go Happy Yourself' is here to help you.

By reading this book it is my hope that you'll be able to have improved relationships with not only yourself, but also your family, clients, employers and customers. You will be able to convey your message in an effective manner at every touch point of your business and career journey. You'll be happy with who you are and also ready to shine your light and provide a legacy for others that find themselves in your world.

This book is broken into 3 parts. We talk about how you step up; we talk about how you show up, we talk about how you stand out when creating your happiness. These are embedded in my 3 pillars of success:

- **Strategy** - you need to know yourself and have a plan of action, set your goals and have a path to follow during this journey that you are going to take.
- **Style** - now this is not only what you wear but how you act and present yourself to elevate your personal brand

and how you use it visually to attract people to you in person and online.

- **Self-care and management** - with us all doing so much, and all the things to make our businesses or careers successful, we often forget to take care of ourselves. Sustainability, in my opinion, is the most important part of the journey.

Now, I'm not going to claim to be a health professional, therapist or counsellor. I'm just going to share some of my experiences, stories, tips, techniques, tactics and routines that I have adopted during my journey of going from busted, broke and burnout to sustainable, stylish and successful on my terms.

So, you may be thinking who is this person, Yvonne Philip aka Yves - The Success Stylist? Well, I am a multi-6-figure award-winning social entrepreneur. I have had it all, lost it all and built myself back up again. I have a portfolio career as an employee, business owner, freelancer and everything in between. I've been on this wonderful planet that we all call home for 50 or so years and I have gained experience and expertise in:

- Careers and business advice
- Project and event management
- Creative production and publishing
- Training and education
- Coaching and mentoring
- Modelling and speaking

I have had an interesting career working and engaging with global businesses such as Universal Music, Hachette Publishing, MACE Constructions, Goldsmiths University and the Home

Office to name but a few. I have met loads of amazing people along the way and obtained a diverse range of experience.

So, why is this book called 'Go happy yourself'? Grammatically it's incorrect but I believe being happy is an action, it's a doing word. It's a verb and it came about when I was in a really dark place in my life. I'd just finished a long-standing relationship; it had been a number of years since I closed down my 6-figure Award-winning social enterprise. I was a single mother, and my son was going through the usual teenage tantrums and troubles that we often have at that age. My mum had migrated back to the Caribbean and fulfilled a lifelong passion and mission of her own. I was in my mid-forties, lonely, confused and not where I wanted to be in my life. I had just started a job a few months earlier in a high-profile charity that seemed to align with me. However, I was snapping at people, and was not showing up effectively at work. I looked like a hot mess, and I was generally leaking bad energy everywhere.

My boss at the time called me into the office and basically broke it down that my behaviour wasn't good enough which led me to burst into tears in the middle of the meeting. She was obviously quite shocked and taken aback as I started telling her what I was going through, how taking on this job with this amazing organisation was a lifelong dream of mine and how I was really hoping that it would get me back on track. That feeling of success and happiness was more than just a job, it was what I craved in all areas of my life.

At this point she turned to me and started to tell me a personal story of her own. A story where she had also broken down because her life was not playing out the way she wanted it and she felt she was giving to everyone else but not herself. The story, although different, was very similar to mine. As a boss, sister and fellow good human, she then went on to tell me the exact words that her mother had said to her.

'Go Happy Yourself!'

That evening I went home and thought about what I could do to 'happy myself' and also where had it all gone so wrong. I also realised that I had been happy before but although I had the strategy and style at the start, I hadn't had the self-care and management and that had affected everything else I did. I didn't have control over the things other people did that affected me, but I realised I could control what I do about it and how I get the success and happiness I want.

So now as you go through this 'Go Happy Yourself' journey, I want you to think about yourself as a holistic being. Happiness can be created in your life, in your career or your business. This book, however, may not provide you with all the answers. What it will provide you with is a lot of questions that you can ask yourself. The answers to which you must take action to create your own happiness.

One of my actions was to retrain as a Personal Stylist. It filled a void. I had a passion for fashion and decided to find a way of merging all of my skills, talents, experience, values and mission into one offer. I now support entrepreneurs and employees to create dynamic, holistic and sustainable personal brands. I achieve this through 1:1 services, online programmes and offline experiences that give my clients the clarity, confidence and credibility they need to succeed and get visible.

Now, you can't be a master of everything, so I have a dynamic team of creatives which include graphic designers, photographers, videographers, web designers, and hair and make-up artists that complement my skills. I take care of the strategy for my clients, providing a one-stop shop for all their personal branding, style and visibility needs. Saving them time, money and emotional stress, whilst gaining the clarity, confidence and credibility to move forward in their careers and businesses.

When you have finished reading this book you will have total personal brand clarity on who you are, your values, your mission, your purpose, your personality and how that fits into your brand and creates a happier life for you. You will be able to then take this information and put it into your style and branding assets and your strategy for success, in person and online. Building on these foundational blocks will be able to make you step up to shine like the star that you are, with the credibility that will attract people to you through speaking, social media and in person connections.

I know that this solution works because I have had lots of other clients I have taken through this process, or who I have worked with as I have been going through my 'Go Happy Yourself' journey. This is what some of them have to say.

> *"Professional, creative, and very business oriented, Yvonne is to the point and is very clued up on her industry. If you want someone who knows what they are doing, and how to get it done, I would highly recommend Yvonne."*
>
> Dr Yvonne Thompson CBE FRSA Chair Radio Academy, Founder/President: WinTrade Week/Economy Honours Committee/Women's Equality Party

'There are only a few things to say about Yvonne Phillip and that is 'she is the best'. No. Scratch that. 'She is the best of the best'. I say this because she always strives for more, always makes sure everyone is happy and always makes sure the experience is enjoyable. Only take her on if you are prepared to truly reach the best you can be."

— CHARLES THOMPSON MBE OWNER, SCREENNATION

"Having worked with Yvonne on several occasions, you learn quickly that she is a woman who just gets things done. Yvonne brings a level of professionalism and clarity that helps to drive a project forward. Knowing Yvonne is on the team is being assured that your project is in good hands."

— JUANITA ROSENIOR MCIPR MIIC MANAGING
DIRECTOR AT MARKETING AND COMMUNICATIONS
AGENCY, TGRG (THE GIRL IN THE RED GLASSES)

"Hey, just wanted to say thank you again for our amazing power session. I had the brand shoot today and I cannot tell you what a difference it made to feel amazing in my own clothes!! Brilliant day after a shitty week, so feeling back on top."

— RACHEL POWER, FOUNDER AND CEO, POWER YOUR
POTENTIAL

Now I'm sure these testimonials of what my employers, clients and co-workers have said about me has made you inquisitive. My big promise to you is that you will be smiling in total satisfaction, total pride, total confidence and total assurance. You will have all you need to implement the solutions that I'm going to give you in this book.

Your 'Go Happy Yourself' journey will start with my first pillar of success and that is having a strategy. Getting clarity on what happiness is and what it means to 'Go happy yourself', where to start and getting out of your comfort zone. We will then move on to exploring and discovering ourselves and who you are as a personal brand - your values, mission, vision, purpose, passions and goal setting for your future.

Pillar two of the journey is creating and showing up in style and with confidence. This includes what you wear, your presence, speaking, social media, photography, video and websites etc.

The third pillar is about growing and sustaining your credibility. This is where the journey takes a slight turn as most people would expect me to write about how to become an author, speaking on stages, event management or getting into the press and TV. These are important for your visibility, but I also know and have experienced two things. A lot of you reading this book have no interest in that kind of visibility. I get it. I was at that stage too at one point. The second thing I know is at this stage of your 'Go Happy Yourself' journey is that self-care and self-management are more important if you are going to be truly happy and not get burned out or overwhelmed.

With this in mind, pillar 3 will support your motivation to keep going, with routines and rituals, tasks on productivity, assertiveness, delegation, problem solving techniques, money mindset and sustainable lifestyle choices. Choices and actions that you need to make because no one can provide the answer to your journey to happiness except you!

This book therefore does not give you all answers to your happiness, but instead guides you through a series of questions that will enable you to find the answers within, thus creating your own happiness holistically.

In addition to this, you will benefit from participating in tasks and reflections to cement your learnings and findings. You may want to grab a notebook or journal and pen to complete these. You will also hear the stories of other women that have been on the 'Go Happy Yourself' journey and are now in a happier place at work and in business. Lastly, you will be able to deepen your knowledge via bonus workbooks, videos, challenges and quizzes which are in the 'Go Happy Yourself' resources area that comes with this book.

So now you know what we're going to cover, are you ready? I would like to invite and empower you to take the next step. Let's get you on your journey to happiness today. Looking forward to seeing you inside.

Love, light and stay true to you.

Yves

PILLAR 1 - STRATEGY

A DISCOVERY AND EXPLORATION TO CREATE CLARITY

1 / WHY HAPPINESS?

Like success, happiness means different things for different people. What makes one person happy does not necessarily mean the same to others. For some it's fame and fortune. However, it is not hard to see, if you look at any celebrity magazine, newspaper or TV interview, that having all the riches does not always bring you joy. For others, happiness is giving back and creating an impact, but giving too much can lead to burnout and a feeling of loss and unhappiness.

'Happying' is the process of discovering the things and actions that bring you joy, contentment, satisfaction, fulfilment and having a wider impact on yourself as well as the wider world. As an experienced businesswoman, career coach and stylist, I would recommend you use this journey to not only create happiness, but really drill down and get clear on where and what happiness you want.

IT'S THE PROCESS OF BEING TRUE TO YOURSELF!

This book will help within the context of your life, career and business success and visibility and how your happiness can affect your personal brand and the way others see you. But how do you see yourself? Are you:

- **Life:** At that stage in your life where you no longer know who you are, and your life seems to be losing focus and purpose. You are in a style rut and not showing up the way you want to.
- **Career**: Stuck in a career rut - Looking to grow a business or change jobs but are not sure if you want to carry on doing the same thing or how to change direction.
- **Business:** You are starting or growing a business and you want to show up as your authentic self and get visible with confidence and ease. However, your fear of visibility is holding you back.

There are many reasons why you may not be happy however, the manifestation of this unhappiness means you are always complaining and being pessimistic. Getting overly angry with the small things. Feeling lonely, hopeless, fearful and often forgetting things. Your insecurities lead you to getting involved in bad habits which further your unhappiness. However, when you are happy, the rest will fall into place. You will be better motivated, inspired and a magnet of goodness.

For example, one of my 'Go Happy Yourself' moments at work was getting not one but two job promotions within 3 years without even asking for one. I was working as an Information

Advice and Guidance Officer trying to rebuild my confidence and get myself back on track. The position was below my skill level and experience but the company was right for me in terms of values and brand. And to be honest I needed to get out of my old job due to the toxic management style. In my new job I was so excited. I smiled and spoke to everyone. I did my work well, however I have to admit within 2-3 months I was getting itchy feet. When I was about 5 months in my manager's manager, the head of department came to me and asked me to organise a major event for the company's clients. She gave me 6 weeks to organise it so things would be tight but I said yes! Despite another person being totally pissed that she had not been asked to organise the event and creating hostility within the department and across the organisation. I couldn't give up on the opportunities to show my worth even if I was not getting paid for it.

I pulled off the event with excellence if I must say so myself. The CEO emailed me to say it was the best event the company had had of that kind. It had really raised my visibility within the workplace.

Within a further 3 month the same Head of Department advised me that there was a new opportunity coming up in the department and asked if I would like to go for it. I applied and got the internal promotion. When she advised me that I was the one the panel had chosen she said it was not only because they knew I could do the job well but my positive, focused outlook at work and my willingness to go the extra mile was why she wanted me.

WHAT HAPPENS IF YOU 'GO HAPPY YOURSELF'?

There are many ways that you can create happy moments. Such as:

- Taking deep breaths and meditating.
- Smiling and appreciating yourself.
- Going outside or spending time with loved ones.
- Putting your phone down and doing some exercise.
- Learning something new and helping others.

But these often only keep you happy for a moment. My mission is to give you the opportunity to be happy for a lifetime by:

- Learning more about yourself and who you truly are.
- Making decisions and plans for your future life, career and / or business.
- Positioning yourself so you can reach your goals.
- Raising your profile and increasing your income and earnings potential.
- Increasing your self-esteem, confidence and clarity on who you are.
- Sustaining yourself and your business in a holistic way.
- Creating a style and way of life that is right for you.
- Creating a career and business that is right for you.
- Living a happier, more fulfilling life.

This book will help you to:

- Find and showcase your strengths so you can stand out from the crowd.
- Tap into your unique skills, talents and passions.

- Leap off the pages and screen to recruiters and customers.
- Take charge of your professional success and stand out while being your best self.
- Find happiness in life and family.
- Elevate your personal brand.

2 / WHAT'S YOUR PERSONAL BRAND AND WHY IS IT IMPORTANT?

When you are considering why branding should matter, you should think about two factors. These factors are the internal and the external elements that may affect your life, career and business.

Your brand is your reputation and the way you are perceived by others. It presents itself in the way you show up, both on and offline, and has the power to:

- Increase job and business opportunities.
- Increase your income and earnings potential.
- Increase your self-esteem, confidence and clarity on who you are.

Now, your brand is more than just lovely pictures and pretty fonts. You need to look deep inside yourself so that you can show up online and in person and present the brand you truly are.

Through my journey to happiness, one thing that has become very clear to me is that we are all a business and brand of one. We can no longer expect to have a job for life. Any change in the economy, world health or poor management of the company you work for can see you unemployed without much notice. On the flip side, as a professional we no longer want to stay in the same position doing the same things for what could be 30 - 40 years.

We all have products and services which we provide as a partner, parent, employee, freelancer or business owner. For the rest of this book, you will hear me refer to those that you interact with as customers, ideal clients, stakeholders, co-workers, children etc. The common denominator is they all want something from you, and you have to interact with them. They will make you happy, confused, frustrated and, at times, make you feel like you want to scream. For us to be happy, we need to be growing, developing and experiencing new things. This means understanding your personal brand.

Those of us with strong, relatable personal brands will have an advantage over those that don't. You will be able to bounce back quickly or transition into something different with ease.

BUT WHAT IS YOUR PERSONAL BRAND?

Many of you may have read the quote;

> *'Your brand is what people say about you when you're not in the room'*
>
> - BY JEFF BEZOS THE FOUNDER, EXECUTIVE CHAIRMAN AND FORMER PRESIDENT AND CEO OF AMAZON.

I personally prefer to explain it as your reputation and the influence you have on others! Let's use some simply math:

What you say + How you act + What you look like = Your Personal Brand

As we go through life, we interact with others online and in person. These interactions create memorable experiences about us and what people can expect from us. When you always deliver on those expectations, you build a strong personal reputation. Delivering your brand clearly and consistently to a wide audience can open up opportunities for you and bring happiness into your life.

Your brand then becomes your personal guide and also a calling card as people know you will deliver a unique promise and authentic representation of you. When building your brand and happiness, you will need to define your individuality. This is all about you and how you maximise your strengths and make choices on how to create future opportunities.

As we go through the process, not only will you learn more about yourself, but you'll also learn about some of the amazing clients that I have worked with, all of whom have taken the path to happiness and come out the other side a more stylish, confident, whole person, in control of their life, career or business. They are achieving their goals on their terms, without apology or overwhelm. But where did we all start our journey of personal and professional discovery? We began with our mindset, being holistic, being honest, getting out of our comfort zone and learning more about ourselves.

3 / YOU AND YOUR COMFORT ZONE

You may feel guilty as you leave the old you behind but let me reassure you, you do not need to leave anything behind. We are discovering a part of you that you have not tapped into as yet, or that you have forgotten as adult life has taken over. This process may also bring up some feelings of anxiety or imposter syndrome about the changes you are about to create, so you will hold yourself back.

These subconscious limiting beliefs all started when we were children, depending on what we were told by our parents, carers, teachers, mentors, peers or the experiences we have been through. Do you remember as a child being told stop, no, don't and you can't! These beliefs unfortunately stay with us. You need to re-create your story as you move forward, and this means your thoughts on you and your abilities too!

You see, these unfounded beliefs formed from the negative words, thoughts and decisions you have built up, held onto and reinforced in life are keeping you in your comfort zone. They are holding you back. You are trapped by the cant's, would haves, should haves and could haves which have or will lead you to fear, frustration and an unhappy and unfulfilling life.

Your comfort zone is like a cage that you live in - a self-created cage that is trapping you. But I want you to remember, you are never stuck! You just keep re-creating the same experiences over and over by thinking and doing the same things. You are maintaining the same beliefs, speaking the same words, wearing the same clothes and doing the same things. So, let's work on this a little. What limits your happiness, success and visibility?

TASK - GETTING OUT OF YOUR COMFORT ZONE

Grab your journal or a notebook and write what is stopping your success and happiness. I have detailed a few to get you started. Can you relate to any of these, or can you add any that are personal to you?

- People will think I am trying too hard or that I am showing off.
- I don't have the money.
- My body is not perfect, and nothing fits me.
- I don't know what to do.
- I don't feel comfortable spending money on myself.
- People should like me for me, not what I look and act like.
- I need to lose weight.
- I don't have the confidence and I am scared.
- I don't deserve happiness.
- I don't like my accent.

Now, for each point you have noted in your journal, I want you to consider the following questions:

1. Why do you think these blocks are true?
2. Are they based on fact or what you have seen / been told and not based on truth?
3. What happened in your past that has made you feel / believe this?
4. On a scale of 1 - 10 how much do you want to get over the blockage?
5. List 5 possible actions that you could take to get over this blockage.
6. Now take action to remove each blockage.

THE POWER OF POSITIVE THINKING

One way you can change your comfort zone is to use affirmations and talking positively about what you have, what you want and acting the way you want to be. To overcome limiting beliefs, you need to flood your subconscious mind with new thoughts, images and wants. You need to start thinking and acting differently. You need to shift your mindset and if you start to follow these steps you will start to see huge rewards.

So, you may be thinking, what is an affirmation? An affirmation is a statement that describes a goal in its already completed state. Here is mine at the start if my 'Go Happiness Journey':

*'I am a woman on a mission with a vision and a passion.
Achieving success and abundance in my life. I am strong,
confident and empowering. I am enjoying my dream job and
business with my ideal clients or something better'*

If you have not done so already, take some time today to think about what is limiting you. What beliefs do you have that are stopping you achieving happiness?

The most effective way to construct affirmations are by using these guidelines:

- Always start with the words 'I am' you have to command who you are and what you want.
- Always use the present tense so it feels that it is already accomplished.
- Affirm what you want, not what you don't want so it is positive.
- Keep it brief and simple so you can remember it easily.
- Make it specific.
- Include a verb ending with -ing so it evokes you doing it.
- Include dynamic emotion or feeling words.
- Make affirmations for yourself not others.
- Add the words 'or something better.'

You can write affirmations on a piece of paper and keep them in your purse, wallet or bag, write them on a mirror, sticky notes or on your phone – whatever works for you. Here are some other ways you should use your affirmations:

- Review your affirmations daily and read them out loud.
- Close your eyes and visualise yourself as the affirmation describes.
- Try to feel the feelings you will feel when you achieve that success.

Let's say goodbye to those limiting beliefs and start creating some new positive happy ones.

You can use the format to overcome a number of blocks you might have. Should you want additional exercises to help you overcome your blocks, visit the additional resources section for this book and check out the Mindset Makeover video, which can be found at: www.yvonnephillip.com/book

4 / WHAT IS YOUR SUPER SKILL?

To develop a strong and clear brand that creates happiness, you need to be clear on who you are. You can then use this clarity to maximise your strengths and super skills and consciously use those to create and guide your future. So, it is time to uncover and define your super skill(s). These are your born talents, your natural ability to do something well. This is the foundation on which your brand and happiness should be built.

Your talent is what you enjoy doing and do the best. This could be something that was identified as a child or through education and development. When you really enjoy your work or do a job well, if you dig a little deeper you will probably find that you were using your natural talents effectively, so it seemed effortless and fun.

I personally love how Psychologist Muhaly Csikszentmihalyi describes this as 'flow'. Flow is when you combine your talents in ways that you find meaningful. Pursuing goals while feeling in control of the process and receiving positive feedback. These 'Flow Experiences' help you identify your talents and show you ways that you can use your talents to find fulfilment and happiness.

The best way to identify your talents and super skills are to look back into your past and ask those who know you well. You must remember however that talents are innate; you were born with them. Some people may call them gifts. Skills can be developed over time, based on your talents. You must continually be developing talents, skills and knowledge for you to satisfy your need for success and happiness. This moves us nicely into our next task.

TASK: IDENTIFYING YOUR SUPER SKILLS

Take a moment to reflect on occasions where you have performed at your best. These can be in different areas of your life, business, career. It's your choice. This is your happiness. Think about your high points and peak performance experiences, moments that gave you a sense of achievement and pleasure. Moments that were meaningful for you.

Jot down 10 - 15 moments in a notepad or journal. When I did this exercise on myself, I initially discovered my strengths were organising and planning, the arts, presentation, performance and helping others.

Now, for each high point, ask yourself:

- Which talent was I using and enjoyed using?
- With what kind of people?
- In what kind of situation?

- Are there any common themes connecting these high points so far?

Answer the following questions about yourself:

- What are the strengths that others acknowledge in me?
- What roles do I fulfil when working as a team?
- When faced with challenges, what are my 'go to' skills to overcome it?
- What was the most successful project I ever completed and what made it successful?
- What was the most important team role I ever fulfilled and why?

Now let's take it a little deeper:

- Did any strengths and skills come up more than once? If so, what?
- Which of these skills excite and motivate you the most?
- What skills do you have but would rather not use as they burn you out?
- What skills are you missing?
- What skills do you need to build and practice?

List your top 7 super skills, starting with the one that gave you the most joy and energy when using it or doing it.

As you go through this exercise, you may identify things that you have forgotten but turn out to be important in your personal and professional growth. As mentioned before, personal branding is not only about you showing up with authenticity and value but also the perception of others. Would they agree with your assessment? Let's find out!

It's time to get feedback from others to confirm your thinking. Ask a friend, professional or others in your community what skills and personality traits you have that sets you apart from others. This could be done in person, via email, social media or a free online survey. It may be a little daunting at first but remember, you need to get out of your comfort zone if you want any form of success and happiness. So go ask a few people and compare their responses to your assessment of yourself.

Another question to ask here is, if none of your high points happened in your current profession or business, are you in the right area? High points provide us with a comfortable bridge to tap into your talents and super skills further. If your high points are in the distant past, is the path you have taken right for you and your future happiness?

REFLECTION NOTES:

Once you have completed the exercise, take a moment to reflect on how you feel.

1. How do you feel about where you have come from?
2. How do you feel about where you are going?
3. What are the underlying themes that you see coming out?

5 / CONQUERING YOUR WEAKNESSES?

We all have things that we don't like to do, struggle with, or that stress us out. I don't like filing, I struggle with writing, grammar and spelling as I am dyslexic (apologies in advance for any typos), and I get totally stressed at the thought of burning out as I have been there before. The effect of stress on your body can be immense. This includes your immune system, your sleep, a drain on your adrenals glands and an impact on your life, relationships, success and ultimate happiness.

Stress is the body's response to threat or demand. The list of demands we go through on a daily basis is endless. It could be business, homework, family, a test, a special project at work, a deadline, an interview, an argument, unresolved conflict, lack of sleep or being late. This list goes on.

We all have different things that stress us out. Some stressors are on-going and can be chronic and predictable. Others are unexpected and life changing. We will be going through some strategic self-management in pillar 3 but I want you to start thinking about the small changes you can make now.

The best way to manage stress is to understand your stress triggers so that you can eliminate them with stress management techniques. Although stressful times are inevitable, it's how you manage them that matters the most.

TASK - WHAT STRESSES YOU OUT?

Look back over the last 12 months and list the key challenges and experiences that have stressed you out. Work out if they were in your control or out of your control, then answer the following questions:

- What are the things you do that cause you stress?
- What are the things other people do that annoy and stress you?

You can be proactive in reducing stress, detailed below are a few things you can do to eliminate unnecessary stress:

- Set the alarm earlier.
- Block out time in your calendar.
- Set clear expectations with people.
- Commit to things that are in line with your values.

Ideas to build your stress coping reserves:

- Make the most of your body's natural cycles of sleep and go to bed early. If you have poor sleeping habits, go to bed 15 mins earlier each night until it corrects itself.

- Have a good evening routine which includes a warm bath or shower, journaling and / or meditation. Make sure your bedroom is optimised for sleep with regard to heat and light.
- Take a walk, move your body and or exercise for at least 30 - 60 minutes a day. This does not need to be at the gym.
- Get fresh air and practice deep breathing. In through the nose and out of the mouth. Repeat at least 10 times.
- Have down time and take a break. It will allow you to come back more alert and focused.
- Eat well and regularly. Junk food just creates brain fog and reduces the ability to think and act clearly. Prepare your food in advance if you have to.

Reducing ongoing stress:

- Be assertive and don't sacrifice your needs to please other people's expectations. It needs to be an 'I'm ok, you're ok' situation. We will discuss this later in the book.
- Develop some sentences that you use when you are under pressure and need some space. For example: "Sounds great, is it ok if I think about it?"

Add some of your own ideas and ask others for tips. Then commit to 3 stress reducing tips for the next 21 days and let's work towards it becoming a habit.

6 / WHAT ARE YOUR VALUES?

It is essential when designing your life, career or business of happiness that it connects with your values and passions. When you live an aligned life of value that includes your passions, you will be excited, engaged and totally unstoppable.

Your values are what you believe to be most important. They show up in everything you do and say. No two people will do things the same, despite having the same talents, as their values will be different. Knowing your values will help you to apply your talents and super skills and build a fulfilling life, business or career. You will know which type of work is right for you. Being true to your values makes you authentic and stand out from the crowd. You will attract customers, colleagues, employers, clients, and / or suppliers with similar values, further deepening your happiness through the right connections.

Let's begin by aligning who you are with what you do and how you do it. It's time to focus on your values and passions before we move on to your purpose and mission. This will allow you to truly show yourself as different to others and showcase your uniqueness. Businesses call it their unique selling point (USP) and as a 'Business of One', we all need to find our uniqueness.

This will help to develop your own road map or follow your internal compass to success and happiness. When developing this map, you need to look at yourself and others for inspiration. Complete these two tasks to find your core values:

TASK - IDENTIFY, DEFINE AND ALIGN YOUR VALUES

PART A - LOOK AT YOURSELF

In addition to the foundations above, I have called your values your personal compass. It provides direction and helps you navigate through your life, business or career. Often, we have lots of values, so we need to narrow our focus down to only a few so as not to confuse others or stress ourselves out. Mine are authenticity, sustainability, and equality. Go through the following exercise to find out yours:

Step 1 - Identify your values

1. Write a list of all of your values. If you struggle with this, visit the resource area for some ideas. You can find it at www.yvonnephillip.com/book
2. Now put an * next to the values that are most important to you.
3. Go through this shorter list and pick your top 5 values, rank them in order in your journal.

Step 2 - Define your values

It is really important that you are clear on what the top 5 values mean to you. That way, you can describe them in a personal and powerful way. Define each of your top values with what it means to you.

Step 3 - Align your values

Carry out a self-assessment to measure how aligned and consistent you are currently living with these values.

PART B - LOOK AT OTHERS

Looking at others can help you access not only what you want to become, but also who you don't want to become. So, let's find your inspiration.

Step 1 - Who do you admire

Write down the names of people you admire. They may be famous celebrities, family members, leaders, neighbours, authors, sportspeople etc, living or not. Produce a list of at least 20 people if you can.

Step 2 - Why do you admire them

Next to each name, write down the qualities and behaviour of their character that you admire in them i.e. confidence, persuasiveness, fitness, enthusiasm, intelligence, honesty etc

Step 3 - How aligned are you with them

Now take a look at the list to see if any themes are emerging. Are there any qualities that are repeated in slightly different ways? Which qualities resonate with you the most. Think about it on a rational, emotional, and spiritual level as these reflect your values. Detail the top 5, starting with most important. Don't forget to detail what this value means to you and also how aligned you are currently to the value in your everyday life and career. If it is important but you are not living this every day, this is an action you need to take to correct as you move forward.

REFLECTION

Wherever you are in life, your work or in your business, can you see why it is right or wrong for you? Is there a mismatch between your work / business and your values? Maybe the work is right, but the people or organisation is wrong. Maybe the organisation is right, but the job position is wrong and therefore making you unhappy.

If you find there is a clash between what you do and your values, it is worth considering a change. The strongest personal brands are built on people doing what they love, in places that are in line with their values.

Select the value or values that are most critical to your success and happiness, but you feel are most out of alignment. Focus on this for the next 21 – 60 days so that it becomes a habit.

If all your values are aligned, think about how you could use your talents and values to move you forward. Look at your list of people you admire for inspiration.

7 / UNLEASH YOUR PASSIONS

When you combine what you are passionate about into what you do, you are more engaged, enthusiastic and inspiring to everyone around you. Now it's time to think about how you can match your passions into what you do whilst connecting them to your career or business goals.

TASK – WHAT ARE YOU PASSIONATE ABOUT?

Let's start by answering the following questions:

- If money weren't an issue what would you do with your freetime?
- What are your favourite activities? If you don't have any, what would you like them to be?
- Why did you choose your university degree / studies / career / business?
- What type of people are you drawn to?

- What volunteering activity or contributions to society do you find interesting and appealing?

REFLECTION

Now, look at your answers and ask yourself the following:

1. Were there any connections or crossovers between your responses?
2. Are you connecting your passions with your studies, business or career goals?
3. How can you do a volunteering (contribution) activity that is in alignment with your passions?

Make a commitment to include your passions into your life, career and / or business plan. It will bring greater happiness to what you do. Make a commitment to yourself that you will include your passions in your day-to-day activities and connect them with your future goals.

8 / YOUR VISION FOR THE FUTURE

Your purpose is your big picture; an internal vision of what you want to achieve in life. When you join clear values which engage your passions and take purposeful action, you should be able to create and follow a personal road map to the place or places you want to go. It is important to visualise what you want and consider what you want to experience out of life, and the impact you will have on the world and those around you if you achieve it.

To find out more about your visions for your future, you can take yourself through a guided visualisation or create a vision board. These will help you on getting clear on where you want to be. It may feel a little awkward at first, but practice makes perfect. My advice would be to just relax, turn off your inner critic and let your mind and imagination do the thinking.

Go to a quiet place where you can be still and undisturbed for at least 20 minutes. There are two full guided visualisations together with a video on creating your vision board in your supporting resources that come along with this book. You can find it at www.yvonnephillip.com/book

GUIDED VISUALISATION PART 1 - WHAT DO YOU SEE IN YOUR FUTURE

Visualise what your life would look like if you had the life of your dreams. Do this for 5 minutes.

What would you say to others about the achievements and the life you are living if you were to reunite with them 25 years after you left school / university? Do this for 5 minutes.

When you have finished reflecting, take several deep breaths, open your eyes and stretch. Once you are fully ready, write down what you will be saying about the life you are leading and the impacts you are having.

Take a moment to capture your key thoughts. Write in the first person with an active voice

"I am.....",

"I will..."

"I have......"

GUIDED VISUALISATION PART 2 - HOW WILL YOU ACHIEVE THIS

Visualise what your life would look like if you had the life of your dreams. There is a knock on the door of the future you. How would you explain your journey to your current self? Detail your notes in the first person:

"I need to be ..."

"I need to do ..."

"I need to have ..."

Jot down what ideas and elements that came out of the exercise.

1. What has been important to you?
2. Who is on this journey with you?
3. What are you doing that fuels your passion?
4. What are you working towards/have you accomplished that gives you a sense of purpose?
5. What do you need to be, do, and have to make it happen?

REFLECTION

Look at your answers. Are your values and passions showing up in your visualisation? What did you learn, if anything? Are there any additions you need to make to your values and passions to ensure you reach your aspirations and future happiness? Do you need additional support, training or guidance to become that better, happier version of yourself?

9 / WHAT'S YOUR MISSION?

We have already mentioned your talents and values as being the foundations on which your personal brand and happiness is built. They are below the surface and determine the size and shape of the building in which your life is being built.

At some point, why you are on this planet is a question we have all asked ourselves. We all have a purpose and sometimes this is confused with a goal or objective. However, a goal or objective is finite and limited, whereas a purpose or mission is infinite and unlimited. We will tackle your goals later in this section but first, let's think about your purpose and mission in a little more detail.

Your purpose is the direction that is right for you. It comes from your super skills and your values. I like the term 'North Star' used by Life Coach Martha Beck. For some people, their purpose only becomes clear towards the end of their life. Many say as long as you feel that you are heading in the right direction, it is all good and you are on the right track. The point is, we should all have a purpose. Some call it their 'WHY'. Why do we want to do or achieve something? This could be for ourselves, our children, family or wider community. That's up to you.

Whatever your 'why' is, it needs to motivate and inspire you to keep going.

Your mission describes how you want to live your life or how you do a job or deliver a product or service. It is important that you understand your mission, or you could find yourself just moving around from one goal to the next without meaning. Like your purpose, your mission is infinite, however it is much easier to define. It is worth taking the time to draft a mission statement rather than just jumping into opportunities. That way it will be easier for you to network and identify opportunities that resonate and benefit you.

TASK - DRAFTING YOUR MISSION

There are many ways to look at your mission and purpose, I prefer taking a two-step approach to it. The beauty of looking at it both ways is that if you find parts that overlap, that sweet spot is your zone of genius and if you can get paid doing it, even better. You will be happy and your pockets will be getting filled - a match made in heaven. So, let's take a closer look.

Think about the following: What is the pain and problem you love to solve? How do you solve it? And how do you convey how your service or the way you do your job will solve it successfully? This method is great if you are considering a career change, promotion or thinking of starting a business.

Step 1 – What's important to you

Take a look at the key areas of life. Are there any areas that are extremely important to you? What are the first questions people always ask for advice about? Rank the key areas of life - 1 being the most important to you, 5 the least important. Then put an asterisk (*) next to the areas that people naturally see you as an expert in.

What are the things that you cannot stop doing or when you do them you get so involved you lose track of time? Athletes call it being 'in the zone'; earlier it was mentioned as your 'flow'. Think back to the talents and super skills you detailed earlier. Ask others for their feelings on this also. What are the things that your friends tell you that you cannot stop doing? If you have not asked them yet, go do it now as it will help you.

- Career
- Finance
- Health
- Social
- Family
- Love
- Recreation
- Volunteering contribution
- Spirituality
- Self-Image

Step 2 – Establish your personal brand area

Choose one area that you are most passionate about as this should be the area of your personal brand. It does not need to be linked to your career however, if not, we could be leaving money on the table so we may need to take a deeper dive into that.

This should give clarity on your personal brand areas, mission and belief statement. These are the principles that help you express your passions and give the right advice with trust and respect. Now, for this step, I want you to write down every belief you have as it relates to the problem you want to solve.

In relation to the problem I want to solve, I believe that

....

Step 3 – Create your methodology

Now it is time to show your credibility, trust and respect by detailing the methodology you used to help people. Think about 2 - 3 times when you have helped someone with the problem detailed above. Break down the steps you used, or process taken to advise them. This is what you will use to show people that you know how to do something and create your personal brand method and mission statement.

Once you have this long form statement you can shorten it into something more succinct and specific.

Examples: This was the mission statement for the social enterprise I founded in the early 2000s:

Our mission is to address the personal, social, health and employment issues facing the community, through arts and creative activities. We achieve this through a programme of:

- Workshops & Training
- Event & Project Management
- Creative Production & Publishing

Belief and Mission Statement 2 - The Success Stylist

Yvonne Phillip, aka Yves, is a Holistic Success and Visibility Consultant with over 30 years' experience of work in the corporate, statutory and charitable sectors. Yves believes that you have to stand out to fit in and not only do you have to stand out to fit in but if women sustain themselves they can sustain the world. So, she helps those who feel stuck and frustrated in their business and careers to get clarity, confidence and credibility with their personal brands and get visible. Yves supports her clients to be uniquely themselves on and offline in a way that represents them and the message they want to send.

Through coaching, courses, 1:1 services, training and experiences that she takes entrepreneurs and employees on a transformational journey to developing and consolidating their personal brand. This includes their strategy, their style and their selfcare and leads them to step up with clarity, show up with confidence and stand out with credibility but without apology or overwhelm. This allows them to make their business fly and they feel fabulous all whilst attracting their dream clients and employers with ease and authority.

PERSONAL BRANDING STATEMENT

Answer the following questions and join them together to produce your statement.

- Who are you: I am...
- What problem do you solve: I solve....

- How do you solve it: I solve this by...
- What do you want them to do/ be/ feel next with this: As a result of working with me they will....

Now you are clear on your mission, your work will be more meaningful. You will have a stronger sense of purpose and be able to build a powerful, happy brand. You need to ensure that you plan goals that fit into your mission and eliminate goals that do not fit. This could mean following a recognised career path, starting or growing a business, or doing things that make more sense to you at that moment in time. Understanding who you are and who you are not is easier once you understand or create your mission. You are on your way to fulfilling your true potential.

People who are described as 'comfortable in their own skin' frequently have a sense of purpose. They are 'at one with the world' and generally attract others who are also authentic. When you have a clear purpose and mission you can communicate it so that others understand who you are and what you do. Those that want what you do, in the way you do it, will be attracted to you. You will also attract people that believe in your mission and want to help you pursue it.

REFLECTION

What steps are you going to take now? Are you ready to communicate your brand and the happiness you want? Don't forget to continue working on your mindset and also to reduce any things that stress you.

10 / ARCHETYPES AND YOUR BRAND

So, you have identified your super skills, values, purpose, vision, and mission. Now it is time to move on to your personal brand identity, or personality, which will express all of them. A distinct personal brand identity will attract the right employers, clients, consumers, customers, partners, friends, colleagues, and consumers to you and also help them recommend you to others.

Your personal brand identity consists of all your branding elements; symbols, signatures, images, colours, fonts, style and how you present them to the world. We will go through some of these in part 2 but before that, I would like to talk to you a little about archetypes for your personal brand of happiness and those that you interact with.

Carl Jung explains archetypes as universal unconscious forms, opinions and images that have the same meaning globally. We all understand and recognise them, even if we do not realise we do. They allow companies and individuals to manage meaning in products, services, and personal brands. It also allows you to create, reinvent, and grow a unique and compelling brand, whatever you do.

Developing a powerful brand involves protecting your purpose and the way it is represented to the world. Archetypes can assist with this. If your behaviour is consistent with your natural archetype, the meaning of your brand will increase, attract, and appeal to people who want what you have to offer.

TASK - WHAT ARCHETYPES DO YOU EVOKE?

Below are 12 different archetypes, together with examples. As we go through them, some may stand out to you, and you naturally evoke its traits and behaviours. You may evoke different archetypes for different situations. For example, at home vs at work or in business. If presented well, it will come to the forefront of people's mind when they interact with your brand. We will come back to how we use this later but before that, go through the list and answer the following questions:

1. Are there any other businesses, media personalities or professionals you identify with each of the archetypes?
2. What archetype do you feel matches your customers, clients, consumers etc.?
3. What archetype(s) do you identify in yourself?

The Caregiver - Is motivated by the passion to help and protect others from harm:

- A healthcare company
- Chemist
- Healthcare workers

- Learning & development staff
- Mother Teresa
- Mary Seacole
- Florence Nightingale
- Johnson & Johnson

The Creator - Have a passion to create and innovate. They have a vision to create that is long lasting:

- Leonardo da Vinci
- Steve Jobs
- James Dyson
- Vera Wang
- Lego
- Sony
- IBM
- Apple

Explorer - Want to discover new things and maintain independence. Naturally curious with science or geography they want to find out more:

- Christopher Columbus
- Marco Polo
- David Attenborough
- Scientists
- The North Face
- Land Rover

The Hero / Heroine - With courage they improve a situation of chaos, standing out as the hero or heroine of a situation:

- Nelson Mandela
- Wonder Woman / Superman
- James Bond
- Tony Robbins
- Police Officer
- Fire Fighter
- Ambulance workers
- Army/ Navy/ Marine Officer

The Innocent - The innocent fosters purity and goodness to create happiness:

- Holy people (Monks, nuns etc)
- Forrest Gump
- Bambi
- Princess Diana
- Anita Roddick (Body Shop founder)
- Innocent Smoothies
- Eco friendly brands
- Dove soap

The Jester - The jester lives in the moment and enjoys a good time. They are highly influential and often say things that no one else would say, as a joke, but this may present other people's prejudice:

- M&Ms
- Sacha Baron Cohen in Borat
- Kevin Hart
- Wowcher
- Ben & Jerry's Ice Cream

- Go Compare

The Lover - Wants to find and give love. They are concerned with staying close to people and finding true happiness, and pleasure:

- Perfume
- Chocolate
- Coco Chanel / Marilyn Monroe
- Fashion models
- Pop stars
- Actors

The Magician - The magician pays attention to hunches and meaningful coincidences to create a transformation:

- Plastic Surgeons
- Cleaning products (Bang and it's gone)
- Robert Kryoasaki
- Harry Potter
- Apple (transforming lives)
- Skincare brands
- Disney

The Ordinary Guy / Girl - Enjoys self-deprecating humour, wants to fit in and connect with others. They do not take themselves too seriously despite possible executive level:

- Stelios Haji-Ioannou (EasyJet)
- Ellen DeGeneres
- Rio Ferdinand
- Robbie Williams

- Walmart
- Primark

The Outlaw - The outlaw is a maverick who rebels and breaks the rules. Disrupts the status quo to reinforce the difference between themselves and others:

- Rolling Stones
- Madonna
- Gordon Ramsay
- Entrepreneurs
- Skype / Virgin

The Ruler - The ruler creates order out of chaos and takes control. They are the people that want to create a successful and prosperous family, company, or organisation:

- Accountants/Finance Officer
- Winston Churchill
- Mercedes-Benz
- Margaret Thatcher
- Anna Wintour
- Sir Alan Sugar

The Sage - A sage helps people to understand the world:

- Plato
- McKinsey
- Morgan Freeman
- Universities
- Publishers
- News channels

None of us fit into a box or just one archetype. On any day, we could evoke a number of different archetypes depending on the situations we find ourselves in. However, one will be prominent, and you will naturally lean towards it. Strong business brands only have one archetype, two at the most. This is because people value consistency and want to clearly be able to identify what you stand for. This also benefits you personally, as you will have a better sense of self and understanding of your behaviours. It presents you as safe, trustworthy, and makes it easier to influence the decisions of others.

If you have more than two archetypes that you can identify your behaviours leaning towards, select the two that best suit the authentic you and make you feel most comfortable. If you are struggling to pin this down, think about your friends, customers and also the celebrities that your values align with.

You do not need to personally evoke the same archetype as your employer or business and may evoke different ones for different tasks and with different people. People are attracted to different archetypes that fit them best, so it may be good to work for or run a business whose values and archetype you strongly lean toward and are also prominent in you. That way, you will be happier in the workplace.

TASK - WHAT ARCHETYPES DO YOU EVOKE

List your top 5 archetypes and then asterisk the 2 that you feel your behaviours evoke the most.

REFLECTION NOTES

Take a look at your values, mission, and purpose. Do they evoke one or more of the archetypes you naturally evoke? Show the descriptions of all the archetypes to 5 friends, family members or colleagues, including people you have known for varying lengths of time. Ask them which archetypes they feel relate to you. If you select the same ones, you have a clear personal brand identity. If you pick different ones, it means your brand is not yet defined. Allow the topics covered already to sit with you for a little while so you gain clarity on who you are and the next steps you need to take on your 'Go Happy Yourself' journey.

11 / SETTING YOUR GOALS

Research shows that the people who write down their goals and review them regularly, earn more than 9 times over the course of their lifetime than those who don't set goals. This means goal setting will allow you to have more impact. To make sure a goal is powerful it must be SMARTER and meet seven criteria:

S - specific

M -measurable

A - attainable

R - realistic

T - time bound

E - evaluated

R - rewarded

Check out the examples below and start to draft your goals:

- I want to lose 2 pounds by June 6th 20xx
- I would like to get a job promotion by March 6th 20xx
- I work as a full time on my business by August 6th 20xx
- I want to look chic and professional for work by 1st December 20xx

You will then need to link it to an evaluation process, so you know it has been achieved, and a reward for yourself when you achieve it. When setting goals, think about what, when, where, why and how. To enhance your goals, you could add the phrase 'or something better'. You will need to set the following:

- Long Term Goals - 5 years or less
- Medium Term Goals - 2.5 years
- Short Term Goals - 1 year
- Immediate Goals / Actions - next 3 months

TASK – GOAL SETTING PART 1

Start by asking yourself the following, the answers should be a lot easier if you have completed the work already detailed in this book:

- What skills, knowledge or experience do you need to achieve this?
- What has worked well for you in the last year?

- What did not work well for you in the last year?
- What does your ideal day look like?
- What were you grateful for in the last year?
- What does success look like for you?
- What were you doing when you were at your best and loving?
- What were your biggest time wasters and stressors?
- When did you have the most fun?

We need to work on the development of the things that went well and bring more of that into your life, business or career, whilst reducing the things that did not go so well or stress you out.

By answering these questions, you will be able to start to visualise the goals. Now, you are probably thinking why is she speaking about visualisations again? It's because when you perform any task in real life, researchers have found, your brain uses the same identical process it would use if you were only vividly visualising that activity. In other words, your brain sees no difference between visualising something and actually doing it.

Visualising your goals can take the form of a vision board, journaling, or exercises. It helps you to understand and commit to WHY you want to achieve your future success and happiness.

- What do you want to create in your future?
- When you imagine completing your goal, what does your life look like?
- What words and phrases represent your life when you've achieved your goals?
- Why do you want to reach this goal?

So, now we have summarised the vision and the mission. We can now focus our attention on what you need to do in the coming year to achieve your medium and long-term happiness goals.

Prioritise your goals based on the 3 things that will make the biggest impact on your happiness, not the 97 other things that will waste your time and energy.

For each big goal, break these down into what you need to do annually and quarterly to reach it. What will your monthly actions, weekly priorities and daily tasks be? How will you know when you have achieved your goal? What are your measures of success and happiness? Most importantly, how are you going to celebrate your achievements and reward yourself? An evening out watching a basketball game with my son, an Afternoon Tea, Spa Day or a night out with the girls are always high on my reward agenda. How will your goals enable you to achieve greater happiness, and what will your rewards be?

TASK – GOAL SETTING PART 2

When you take time to celebrate your achievement, in whatever way you like, it is also time to take stock on how well you have done. It provides a time for you to review your progress and plan the next stages of your journey to success and happiness. So, ask yourself:

- What incredible things did you make happen over the last year / quarter/ month/ week?
- What did you or are you going to do to celebrate?

- What are you grateful for over the last quarter?
- How do you feel right now?
- Is there anything you'd like to change going forward?
- What are your goals for the next quarter?

Please note that it's not enough to simply write your goals down and expect them to be wished into existence. You will need to take inspired action. Please ensure that you also:

- Review your goals 2 or 3 times every day.
- Take time to read the goals out loud.
- Visualise and picture the goals as if you have already accomplished them.
- Take time to feel as if you have already accomplished each goal.

To achieve a big goal, you are going to have to become a bigger person. You must develop new skills, new attitudes, and new capabilities. This will come by not only taking action, but also addressing your self-limiting beliefs and getting support when needed. This support could be from mentors, coaches, partners, therapists, counsellors, accountability buddies, master minders, or through community.

If you still need support with setting your goals, you can access my 5-day Goal Setting like a Goddess challenge in the resources that accompany this book. You can find it at:

www.yvonnephillip.com/book

12 / DISCOVERY AND EXPLORATION YOUR STRATEGY IN ACTION

Rachel Power is Career Confidence Coach, championing disheartened professionals and clients. She left her 20-year career to pursue her talent and discover happiness. I sat down with her to discuss her transition and advice to others looking to change careers or get internal job promotion.

Yvonne

Hi there, Rachel, and thank you so much for agreeing to be interviewed for this book as one of my clients, and also somebody that I really respect in the career coaching space. So, as you all know, I do support people with their careers. But I start with people at the beginning of their career, where you actually help people that are mid-career to make that change. You have also been through a career transition yourself and stepped into your brand as a personal brand, rather than an employee. So, the first thing I wanted to ask you, Rachel, is what made you step out as your own brand and change your career? What was that point that you got to, that said, "Enough is enough?"

Rachel

Well, where do I start? I was 20 years in the same procurement job. And it's funny, because when you talk about personal branding, I've read a lot about personal branding over the years. But I didn't really know what my personal brand was. And in hindsight, I think that was locked into the fact that I don't think I was in the right job for me. I knew the importance of personal branding, but I didn't do it, because I didn't really know where I fit. So, to the question "what was it that made me do it and make the change?" It was actually when I was told that the leadership team had decided that I had "reached my potential". And it was a bit like, "hmmm I don't think so".

That was actually quite a trigger to me, to make me want to do something about it. The boss that I was working for at the time very much held me to account. She gave me this nudge of feedback which really sent me on a journey of self-discovery, which is something that I'd avoided. The basic stuff such as, what are your strengths? What are your interests? What are your values? I dived into those and I came to the conclusion that I was a coach. What was funny was that everybody around me was like, "yeah, that's pretty obvious". But it hadn't been obvious to me. I'd been doing it over the years, but I didn't recognise or acknowledge that I was doing it.

Yvonne

Absolutely. And I think that is what a lot of people find - they're working in a job where they're comfortable. They know their job, they know the company, they know what to expect. They're getting that regular salary every month, so they feel comfortable, and it's secure. But they're not actually, as your boss told you, fulfilling their potential.

Rachel

Yeah, it's, it's funny you say that, though, because I knew, deep down in my heart, that I was in the wrong place. I used to research every job going, and I used to discount everything "Well, no, I'm not that. And I'm not that and I'm not that"

Yvonne

So, your limiting beliefs started coming in, which stopped you from moving forward and kept you in the comfort zone?

Rachel

Yeah, but I was almost running away, rather than running to, because I wasn't focusing on what I really wanted. I didn't ask myself the questions - What are your strengths? What are your values? What are your interests? Actually, if you really focus on that, the answers are all there for you.

Yvonne

100%. This book starts with that process of understanding who YOU are. Because once you understand who you are, it's so much easier to step into your personal brand, because it will dictate all the other branding elements. Did actually knowing who you are and other people validating that, give you a boost of confidence?

Rachel

Yeah, I think it did. When I worked with you on the style work we did. I'll never forget it when you said to me that even my house was all on brand. All of this stuff - it was there! I just didn't know. I even worked with a guy on my website who came up with the green and the yellow branding colours and I was like, "Oh, yeah, they're me." It felt like I was coming home.

Yvonne

It was an amazing process! It was so easy because you understood what you wanted. All I needed to add was a splash of pink. You had the colours there, the yellow and the green. I just added a splash of pink, and I was like, "Bam! that is you!" It was so easy to dress you.

Rachel

Yeah, but I've never put it all together and that's what was weird to me. So, I've got this career where everybody else can see it and I can't. I've got a house that's my brand colours and I don't even know they're my brand colours. It's funny because you say it was easy, but at the same time, it was a real epiphany for me. When I put that outfit on with the pink jacket.... I was just looking at myself going, "Oh, my God, like, Yeah, this is me". It was all in the cupboard and I had never put them all together. It made me feel complete. At the beginning, I said how I understood the importance of having your personal brand, but I never had one because I didn't really know who I was. After our session, it all just slotted into place. It really does come back to knowing your strengths, your values, your interests and who you really are.

Yvonne

Yes, also what mission are you on, because a lot of people that find themselves stuck in their career don't know what they want and who they are, so they're just applying for jobs and finding themselves in roles where they're with companies that don't align to their values. In this book, I don't want to persuade people to become entrepreneurs if that is not for them. I just want people to be able to step into who they are, because they're gonna get a lot more success out of their life, their businesses, and their careers if they do. So, I'm really glad that you had that epiphany. It came so easily to me - this is who you are, this is your brand and how you need to represent it. That is my zone of genius. For others, it can be hard to come to the forefront.

Rachel

Yeah, but it just goes back to that point, though, doesn't it? That's your zone of genius. I really believe everybody's got their genius. They just don't know it or haven't realised it yet.

Yvonne

Absolutely - and yours is about coaching, where you created Power Your Potential. When I heard the name of your business, I was so excited. I was like, "Yes, that's the one." You said that your boss told you that you were not reaching your full potential, and then your name is Rachel Power. A great combination of your moment and who you are.

Rachel

Yes, that is how I felt. I brainstormed loads and when Power Your Potential came up, I was like "Yes, yes. That is the one."

Yvonne

That is a great example of those lightbulb moments that you have as you're going through a personal brand process. So, you mentioned that your boss told you that you weren't reaching your full potential? You've now moved into running your own business and you're no longer working for that company. Did you have any challenges as you were going through this career transition? What would you advise other people that may be thinking about changing their job, or starting a business, to start thinking about as they're going through that career transition?

Rachel

Interesting question. I think people are key. Even though I work for myself, I feel like I've got a stronger network than when I worked in an organisation with 100,000 people. It's key to find your tribe, having a role model and realising that there are groups of people out there that are like you. Finding people whose values align to yours, role models, people who can coach and mentor you and hold you to account, I think that's really key. I was brought up to believe that help was a weakness, and this had me stuck for so long. I believed you should never ask for help. I was stuck for a long time, never really asked for help, never really told anyone my dreams. So, my advice would be to start connecting to the right people for your purpose. So, if your purpose is to learn to have a business, then you need to surround yourself with people who've got their own businesses and people that you can learn from.

Yvonne

Yeah, I would advise the same in terms of getting yourself within those networks, whether it be business or employment networks, letting people know what you're good at and what you want to do. We're social beings, we want to help others, but they can only help when they know what you want to do.

Rachel

Yeah - that's such a powerful point. One of the books I was reading at the time of discovering myself, by Barbara Sher, has a saying "isolation is the dream killer". It's so true to life. Trying to do this on your own will never really make it happen as much as we all think. If you think about the top people in business and sport, it's all about coaching, mentoring, and surrounding yourself with other successful people.

Yvonne

Absolutely. In addition to following your networks and making sure you put yourself out there, is there any other advice?

Rachel

I think if you are at the start of your journey then you need to start exploring things. You don't know what you don't know. Don't be scared to explore things. The job market today is very different now than when I left university. The world is changing. Whatever your background is, whatever your parents have done, or whoever has been your role models as you're growing up, you need to try and broaden your horizons and just see what else is out there. There's never been a better time to explore.

Yvonne

For those mid-career changes, would you advise them of the same thing? Or is that slightly different? Because they've obviously got a little bit more of a track record behind them?

Rachel

People at this stage tend to think that if they do something else now, they're losing everything and have to start over. And that's not true. You're not starting over from scratch, you're not green or wet behind the ears. You have x number of years of experience and transferable skills, and whatever industry you've been in, the fundamentals are transferable. If you're a people person, and you can build relationships, that's not confined to whatever area you have been in.

So, you can climb a ladder and go up in terms of promotion, or you can think about how you can build a portfolio career based on going wide. And think, what transferable skills do I have that can support another industry or another job sector? Or what am I really passionate about doing next?

And why are you doing it? Growing up you get told to work up the ladder. But do you want to go up the ladder? Are you wanting to lead a team with loads and loads of people? Do you want that people responsibility?

Yvonne

Absolutely. That is what you're told to do! You start at the bottom, you become a supervisor, then you become a manager, then you become a director. But a lot of people just don't want to do that.

Rachel

Yeah. If you're passionate about people - and I really do believe the best leaders are people that care about people - and you lead from empathy, then be a leader. But I don't necessarily see that as success. Ask yourself, what does success look like to you? Success is different to different people, and you shouldn't judge and compare. Actually, that is another piece of advice. Don't compare yourself. The only person you should compare yourself to is yourself and how you were doing yesterday.

Yvonne

Yeah, you are on your journey. And you've got to make your life a success on your terms, whatever that means. If we all had the same definition of success, life would be very difficult and we wouldn't succeed, because there'd be too much choice out there. Being different and how you differentiate yourself through your brand, and your personality is what's going to attract people to you. It's what's going to make you stand out.

Rachel

Yeah, absolutely, knowing who you are and being clear to others about who you are. Another thing we do is comparing ourselves and always seeing what we don't have, rather than what we do and deciding we're not really good enough.

Yvonne

Yes, you're always thinking about that negative, so you're attracting negativity to you. Instead, you should be thinking "What's great about me? What can I add to enhance that?"

What I would also add in terms of your brand's transition is to think about a portfolio career and doing lots of things that make you happy. That's how I've got to where I am now. There are loads of people like, " Yvonne, you've done film, you've done modelling, you've written for a magazine - what haven't you done?" I've just done things that have interested me, and it's now led me to have such a wide holistic brand, that I'm just totally in my zone of happiness.

Rachel

I love that Yves, and you have reminded me of Barbara Shear, the same author I mentioned earlier. Another book she has is "Refuse to Choose." That was an aha moment for me because again, from school you 're told to choose a career and that is it for life, when in fact, it isn't! Follow what you're interested in. You don't have to choose one thing forever, but you do have to make decisions otherwise you will end up doing nothing.

Yvonne

You started your business about six months after you decided that you were going to do that, how fearful were you in terms of stepping into that? Okay, you've had 20 years, with 1000s of employees, the HR department and the additional perks - how fearful were you to step out on your own? Or because of the community and the support that you had around you with the training and the coaching, did you feel comfortable stepping out as your own brand?

Rachel

I don't think I was scared because it worked out. Because I've gone through this process of who are you? What are you about? It kind of felt like, "I've got to do this." It was more scary for me to stay where I was in that comfort zone, than to go and do what I needed to do. It's interesting, because I've been coaching a couple of ladies who are in their late 50s and they're at the same point. They're like, "I can't stay - I am more scared of staying stuck than I am to move to this unknown world." And it's such a satisfying feeling because you don't want to get stuck.

Yvonne

It is not a nice place to be - in stone. And I absolutely love the fact that you were like, "Yeah, I was fearful - but I had to do it for myself." You didn't want to be unsatisfied for another 20 years and then retiring after having an unfulfilled life.

Rachel

Yeah, one of the things I always say to clients is, "What will you regret?" We're all on this planet for a small space of time - and we don't know when that time is up. The only thing we know is that at some point, we're all good to go. It's like well, what will you regret? When you're on your deathbed, what would you wish you'd done? Those are the things you should be prioritising right now.

Yvonne

Absolutely. As your brand, how do you wish you would have shown up? There's no reason that you can't be showing as yourself within your authentic being.

Rachel

Yeah, and I think that it's really good that you look at it that way, because we talked earlier about not comparing yourself, but at the same time, if someone else can do it, so can you! There's no reason any of us can't if we put our mind to it. It's very easy to be the victim. You choose - it's a choice.

Yvonne

As far as I am concerned, our brands are ever evolving. Our parents are from the era of getting a job and staying there for life, whether you were happy or not. I have always been able to pay the mortgage and put food on the table, but I am doing what I feel is right for me. I don't want anyone that reads this book to have regrets later on in life that they didn't do what they really wanted to do.

Rachel

Yeah, building on that, I would never recommend someone to resign recklessly. If you really hate your job, get a good financial plan behind you. It is not one or the other. Make a plan and don't keep suffering! One thing I became more aware of since coming into the entrepreneur world is how many people are doing a side hustle. You can get the stability from your corporate job and build a side hustle to test and explore. Cake baking, photography and social media services - so many options! It's not 1950 anymore.

Yvonne

Yes! What side hustle ideas can you develop out of a hobby that you can build a personal brand from? There are so many different skills and experiences that you can build up part time.

Yvonne

When you were employed, you didn't feel like you had a brand. However, when you went and you questioned people about their thoughts and feelings for you, I think nearly 100% of them came back with the same thing. Is that right?

Rachel

Yeah, and I think I was too busy comparing myself to what I wasn't. So, I knew what I wasn't, which is actually how I got into procurement. I knew I wasn't going to do finance and I knew I wasn't going to do marketing and I came across procurement. "Oh yeah, that'll do!"

Yvonne

Your brand is what you say, how you act and what you look like. What was beautiful about that is that everybody had the same feeling about you - but you just didn't identify with it.

Rachel

Yeah, I did not piece the whole thing together. All the pieces are there but you can't always see them. Sometimes you need someone to hold the mirror up.

Yvonne

In terms of careers, I would advise people to build a strong brand at work, especially if you're looking to get promotions. Doing good work, networking, and showing up in the right places and letting people know what you want. Also making sure your worth work ethic is 100% spot on. Would you add anything else to that?

Rachel

The first thing that came to my mind was visibility. You can be doing all the great work in the world, but if nobody knows about it, you're not gonna get anywhere.

Yvonne

Yeah, absolutely. It is about raising your visibility and making sure the bosses know what work you're doing. Anything else you want to add?

Rachel

Self-confidence. This is a known stat, that for women that's often harder than for men. We know that women are brought up to not necessarily be the people to be shouting about their achievements and actually actively told not to. But you have got to find a way to learn strategies that work authentically for you. If you don't believe in yourself, nobody else is going to believe in you. Sometimes you might have to do some deep work that's uncomfortable. I actually did six weeks of hypnotherapy, to get rid of some gremlin stuff that I had going on. Once I was aware of it, I had to choose to face it, or nothing was going to change.

Yvonne

You've got to be the change in your own life. You can't expect anybody else to do that for you.

As women we often don't apply for jobs because we can't do everything that's in the job description. However, you know, it's a statistical fact that if men can do 50% of the job, they're applying for it. So, we need to change that mindset and build the confidence to say, "Okay, I can't do 25%-50% of this job application. But from a learning and development point of view, I will take the training courses and train myself to be able to do those things and be totally transparent about that".

Rachel

Yeah, totally. It's funny because you say it's the difference between men and women. I actually coached a guy who wasn't going to go for a particular job because he didn't have the formal qualification, but he had loads of experience and was really suited to this job. I told him to go for it and tell them everything he did have to see where he got to. It was so exciting because he got the job! Now he's like a different person. He had been in the wrong environment in the wrong type of work which was making him miserable. But now he's doing this thing that he was always capable of, but he nearly didn't do it! So, I think it goes back to holding the mirror up, and just repackaging and reframing things that you don't necessarily see about yourself.

Yvonne

Now you have been through a career transition, setting up your personal brand and working for yourself, how are you feeling?

Rachel

I feel like I have found myself. I feel like it is right.

Yvonne

And that is where we need to get everybody to. Where they are feeling right about who they are and how they are showing up. Just doing that one thing will lift up your confidence. Yes, you may have to do some inner work to get there. You can grow your career, grow your business and create your personal brand. You can really own your stuff and unapologetically be you, which will in turn attract the right people to you.

You mentioned having support networks and communities and I am sure that once you knew who you were, you knew the right people for you and how to find them!

Your career transition has been such an achievement.

Rachel

That's the beauty of coaching. Once you get the clarity, it flows, and you can make decisions much easier.

Yvonne

Once you know your brand and who you are, that helps your decision-making process. You know your strengths, values, vision, mission, and passion, so you can ask yourself, "Is this on brand?"

Rachel

Again, that increases your self-confidence as when you don't have that clarity, it makes you doubt yourself and you can't guarantee you will make the right choices.

Yvonne

Going back a little bit, did you find that when you were employed you followed your employers' values and their brand?

Rachel

Where I worked, the company values were very similar to mine. When I think about my personal branding and my visibility, my whole strategy was to stay under the radar. It goes back to my lack of self-confidence and that I didn't really feel like I fit in. I would get the work done, became known as a safe pair of hands and never said what I thought. I made myself invisible. I think, deep down, that was because I knew I didn't want it.

Yvonne

It became a self-fulfilling prophecy. You were stuck.

In terms of the visibility piece - you are so visible now! You have really come into your own!

Rachel

With hindsight, it was quite obvious really. But I was scared, and I didn't ask for help.

Yvonne

And you know what? It is ok to be scared but it's not ok to stay stuck.

Rachel

And to come full circle, it's not ok to not ask for help. If you never say that you need help, no one is ever going to help you. You need to admit it to yourself first.

Yvonne

Absolutely. You have to be true to yourself and be honest and hold that mirror up.

Before we close, what do you think you have enjoyed the most out of this whole styling, branding and visibility process you have been on?

Rachel

All of it! There is nothing I haven't enjoyed! I have really enjoyed testing and exploring. I get braver every day. I have really strong foundations, which I can thank you for, and that has given me the confidence to play, explore and have fun with it all.

Yvonne

Good luck in the next stage of your brand success! I have no doubt that you are going to be amazing as your brand is so strong! I have never seen anything like it. It is just you and you are unique.

Rachel

When you find it - it is amazing!

Yvonne

Go for that promotion, become the brand that you want to become and go for what you really want to do.

13 / THE ACCIDENTAL PAY
RAISE

With the above interview in mind, you will remember at the start of this pillar I mentioned that I got two job promotions within 3 years without even asking. Well I told you one of the stories which was all about being a magnet to success and happiness. Now, I think it's time I told you about the other promotion.

The event I organised was about celebrating diversity, a topic that is not only close to my heart in terms of my values around equality but as a black women a topic that I face daily in terms of race and gender. I joined a number of sector groups on race equality and supported events with David Lammy MP, Marvin Rees MP and other thought leaders on the topics. I even chaired the launch of a new funding stream to support Black History activities throughout the year and not just in October when it is celebrated in the UK.

I was also invited to become the Chair of a newly formed staff forum and work. A formal group set up by the company to hear staff views on topics that affect them in the workplace. Now either of these were part of my role but was needed within the organisation so I agreed. This saw me attending meetings with the CEO and executive team and within 6 month new policies and procedures were implemented with the organisation based on our reports, requests and recommendations. I soon became the go to person within the organisation for EDI (Equality, Diversity and Inclusion). Not something that I have in my plan but something that was meaningful for me.

Then one day my manager emailed me and advised that the company had given me a pay rise. They wanted me to lead on resident EDI engagement officially. Just like that they were acknowledging my work, natural ability and rewarding me for it.

Now I can't say that everyone will have the same opportunity as me. Most of us will have to ask for a pay raise if we want something more than the average 1 – 5% given annually if you're lucky.

Take on extra projects that are in line with the things you have discovered about yourself so far in pillar 1. You can no longer think just because you have been there the longest that you will be automatically given the job.

Raise your profile within the organisation to show your worth. Produce content, come up with ideas, suggestions and activities. If you see something that needs doing, take the lead and see what can be done about it.

Note the value of this extra work to the organisation in terms of finances and reputation. You will need to present your thoughts, facts and feelings to the company at a meeting or presentation. If you cannot clearly articulate this the company will not accept your request for a pay raise or promotion. When and if you have a meeting with your manager about this it's what will make or break your request.

If they say no, don't despair. You are on their radar and there is one of three things that you can do:

- You can start looking for another job with a higher salary.
- You can continue as you are and try again in say 6 months.
- Start your own business on the side to create the extra income.

Knowing the reason why your request has been denied will influence your decision and next step so make sure you find this out.

REFLECTION

What could you do and what goals and actions could you set to get a promotion or make a change in your career?

Will you take on additional projects at work that will not only support your learning and skills development but also make the workplace a better one by increasing staff morale or the business bottom line?

PILLAR 2 - STYLE

DESIGN AND CRAFT YOUR CONFIDENCE

14 / WHY STYLE MATTERS

Now you have the clarity on who you are and the direction you are going in, it's your time to share that with the world, in whatever way is right for you. Now it is time for you to start showing it through your style.

Your style is often the first element of your brand to present itself as being unhappy and the last thing you think about when trying to create happiness. I feel that it is the element that brings what is inside of you out and presents it to the world.

Now, despite one of my super skills being that of a personal stylist, when I talk about style, I am not just talking about what you wear but also how you act and present yourself. It's the way you do things. Your Personal Brand in action!

Now, my wish for you is that you can show up with the utmost confidence in who you are and slay every interaction you have with ease, authority and authenticity. Finding your style will help you along the way. In this section we will first look at the elements of your style you wear and later on in the section we will look at how you act, before moving on to how you show up online and offline. Collectively, we will call it your personal impact!

When you are considering why style should matter, you should think about two factors. These factors are the internal and the external elements that may affect your life and style.

Internal Factors - If you wear the same type of outfits all the time, it can break down your self-esteem and confidence. It can make you more self-conscious about your body and how to dress it to show yourself off in the best light. There are a million ways to enhance your body image, but style is a great way to not only enhance your own path to self-love and happiness but also the way others may see you.

External Factors - Our appearance and image have a huge impact on how we are perceived by friends, family, colleagues and society. Our lasting impression of someone we meet is decided within the first 3 - 7 seconds, with 55% of this opinion made up by visual appearance and actions. It is my aim to ensure you feel empowered to be the very best version of yourself always.

These 7 seconds could be the difference between you:

- Meeting the partner of your dreams!
- Securing the job, promotion or client you have always wanted!
- Or just simply having the confidence to embark on the next chapter of your life!

TASK

Let's review your style in terms of what you wear to see if it is holding you back. Answer the following in your journal:

1. On a scale of 1 – 10, how easy is it to dress each morning?
2. On a scale of 1 – 10, how happy are you with your outfits?
3. How would you describe your current style in 3 words?
4. Do you think these words properly describe or represent your personality?
5. What outfit is your favourite and why?
6. Which outfit is your least favourite and why?
7. What types of garments do you wear the most?
8. Which colours have you worn the most?
9. Do the clothes fit you well?
10. Did you feel overdressed or underdressed at any point in the last week?
11. Did you receive any complements in the last week?
12. How comfortable do you feel in the outfits?
13. What message are you sending out about yourself in these outfits?
14. If money, time and confidence was not an issue, would you wear these outfits?

With goals being so important to the future of your success and happiness, it is important to get them written down to assist with clarity and direction. So, let's take some time to think deeper about what you want to be, do and achieve with your style and personal impact by answering the following questions:

1. Why do you want to change and update your style?
2. What will success look like once you have finished the process?
3. What do you like about your current style and would like to keep?
4. What do you dislike about your current style and need to change?
5. What aspect of your style needs the most work?
6. Have you done anything to try and change your style? If so, what?
7. Will anything happen if you don't improve your style? If so, what?
8. What are your goals in your personal life?
9. In what timeframe do you want to achieve this?
10. What will success look like when you get there?
11. What do you most desire with regard to changing your style?
12. Are there any skills you would like to learn? If so, what?
13. Are there any trends you would like to learn about and / or try?
14. What style types speak to the sense of dress you want?
15. What message to the world do you want to project when it comes to your style?

Think back to what you have learnt and discovered about yourself and the way you like to do things so far. Take some time today to set 3 style goals for yourself that will support this.

15 / WHAT TO WEAR FOR
YOUR SHAPE

As women most of us dislike some part of our body or another. Some of us think we are too fat, others too thin. Our bums, our tums, our boobs and our legs, everything seems to be in question. I personally don't like that I have an extremely flat chest and yes I could go under surgery but that would go completely against my values of authenticity. Your body shape does not define you as a person and my feeling on the topic is, as long as you are physically and mentally healthy that is what should matter the most. It should not be what the media, celebrities and others say our bodies should look like.

Speaking of celebrities, some famous people communicate their purpose and archetype through their style, and you don't have to be any different. You can do this by following a dress code, style type or creating your own individual sense of style.

With style you can also evoke an archetype, for example:

- Creator - original clothing and unusual hairstyles.
- Ruler - strong suits or expensive accessories.

- Outlaw - not conforming to dress stereotypes.
- Jester - T-shirts with cheeky quotes.

You need to think about your style and the message you want to communicate through it. But first we need to think about the cut and silhouettes of garments and accessories that suit you.

YOU AND YOUR BODY SHAPE

Did you know that in a study, 9 out of 10 women didn't really know what body shape they were? Many of them mistakenly thought that they had a proportional / hourglass body shape. This ultimately means that they are dressing wrong for their body and not showing up in the best way they can.

I remember when I first became interested in personal styling and image consultancy in the 1990s, I came across 9+ different body shapes. It was all just a bit confusing for me as a consumer. I now work within the five main body types and use my super skills to adapt based on the client.

Proportional / The Hourglass - Deemed the perfect body shape, you could be slim and petite or full and curvy. Your body shape is well portioned with your upper and lower body being equal with a well-defined waistline. If you have this body shape you are lucky enough to gain or lose weight evenly throughout the body. The cut of the clothes needs to mirror your figure to show off your curves and accentuate your feminine shape. The aim is to highlight your waistline and avoid any boxy shaped clothing. Pointed shoes, chunky heels, ankle boots, and knee-high boots always look good on the hourglass body shape.

The Heavier Bottom / Pear Shape - The pear body shape is the most common female body shape. Your upper body is straighter, more angular and smaller than your lower half which is fuller and curvier. Most ladies with pear shapes have defined waists and a smaller bust. Your aim when dressing is to balance the upper body with the lower body whilst emphasising your waistline. This means broadening the appearance of your shoulders through style and detail such as patterns, prints, frills and ruffles etc. Heels to lengthen the body, peep toe, and boots that cut off just below the knee suit this body shape the best.

The Slender / Rectangle - If you have a straight up and down body shape with no real defined waist, you have a rectangle shape. There is no significant difference in terms of size between the upper, waist and lower measurements. Often referred to as having athletic or boyish figures. There are two versions of this body shape, one being lean and straight the other fuller and straight. You can wear most clothes. If you are lean, you could benefit from breaking up the body to create curves and a waist. Slender body shapes look great in stilettos, ankle or calf high boots, and ballet flats.

Heavier Top Half / Inverted Triangles - Inverted triangles have wide shoulders, broad backs and can have a full bust but from the waist down have a small waist, narrow hips and slender legs. Your broad shoulders are your asset as they will make your waist look smaller. The aim with this body shape is to balance the lower body with the upper body using the correct styles below the waist. Flared and A-line skirts or peplum tops are great for this. This body shape looks good in delicate and slim heels, stilettos, or brightly coloured heels.

The Full Figure / Apple Shape - The apple body shape is fuller on the upper body with a prominent stomach and fuller waistline. The aim is to emphasise the shoulders and keep the focus on the neckline, face and away from the stomach area. You can do this by raising your waist to the empire line and allowing the fabric of your garment to flow loosely over your larger areas. Wedges and chunky shoes, strappy sandals, ballet flats, and calf length boots look great on this body shape.

FACE SHAPES ANALYSIS AND IDEAL GLASSES, HAIRSTYLES, AND JEWELLERY

There are 7 different face shapes, once you have identified your face shape you can determine what glasses frames, jewellery and hair styles work for you. The 7 face shapes are Oval, Square, Round, Oblong, Diamond, Triangle and diamond.

Like your body shape, it's all about focusing and enhancing those beautiful characteristics we have and hiding the ones you don't think are so great! Just remember you are absolutely beautiful in any case.

The Round Face Shape - The round face shape has prominent, rounded cheeks with the width and length of the face being equal. Round faces can be hard to accommodate, but all is not lost. What you need to do is to make your face appear longer and leaner.

To do this you'll need a haircut with less volume around the face. Avoid chin length bobs, centre partings, and choose hairstyles that add height to the top of your head. A shoulder length haircut, with soft graduated layers is your ideal style. You can have bangs/ a fringe if you like, but keep them long with a side parting. People with a round face shape should look for glasses which contrast their face shape. These include rectangular and narrow frames that will shorten the face. With jewellery choose styles that are longer than they are wide.

The Oval Face Shape - People with an oval face shape have a naturally proportioned face. However, their forehead may be slightly wider than their chin, and the length of the face is about one and a half times the width. This is deemed the ideal face shape and although most frames and jewellery will suit this shape, ones that are wider tend to suit you better.

There are no limits to the hairstyles for your face. You can pull off nearly anything from long to short lengths, layers, bangs / a fringe, blunt cuts, angled ends. If you have great bone structure, try a short angular bob that shows off your chin!

The Inverted Triangle Face Shape - A triangle face shape is widest at the forehead and narrows quite steeply down to the chin. The chin is pointed, unlike the more rounded heart shape. Frames with detailing on the upper portion are ideal. Ensure the width is slightly wider than the jawline. Cat eyes frames work well. You can use waves and curls to soften and widen your jawline. Layers around the face will also work well. Earrings that are longer than wide are good as they narrow the jawline.

The Square Face Shape - A square face shape has a prominent angular jaw and square chin, with your forehead and jawline roughly the same width. If you want to soften the look, someone with this shape should avoid angular frames and opt for rounded, rectangle or oval shaped glasses so as not to accentuate the squareness.

When choosing hairstyles, you will need to add height to the top of your head. Movement at the temples and side will soften your bone structure. The best hairstyle for your facial shape is something with a lot of texture. Curls or choppy ends or even short spiky cuts. Avoid blunt cut bangs/fringes and one length bobs. Light layers will soften your face shape as will curls or a side parting. Choose jewellery styles which will sit close to the face and slim the jawline.

The Oblong / Rectangle Face Shape - Often confused for the oval face, an oblong face will have a longer shape that is not as wide as an oval and often has a narrow chin. If you have this face shape, avoid narrow or small square shaped frames as they could make your face look longer and angular. Wider frames are good and frames with a prominent bridge over the nose will break up the length of the face.

Hairstyles that add fullness to the side of your face work best. Those with long face shapes should try adding some width to your do, such as blunt bangs/ fringes, and chin length bobs. You just want to be careful to not add more length that will drag your face down. If you have long hair with a long face, have a fringe/bangs cut in. Avoid long jewellery, straight hair and height on the top of your head as this will elongate your face.

The Diamond Face Shape - Characteristics on a diamond face shape include a narrow forehead and jawline with cheekbones at the widest point of the face. To highlight and soften the cheekbones, frames with detail or distinctive brow lines are best. This includes oval and cat eye frames. A fringe / bangs will add volume to your forehead. You could add volume to your temple and jaw line with curves and curls. Once again avoid long jewellery styles.

The Heart Face Shape - A key feature of this face shape is that it has a wider rounded forehead and cheekbones with a narrow jawline and chin. If you have a Heart/Diamond face, draw the focus more to your eyes and cheekbones. This face shape can suit both angular and round glasses. Avoid glasses that are wider at the top than the bottom as this will make the face look top-heavy.

Fringes / bangs will soften a wide forehead. Go for earrings that add width to your jawline. Try a side swept fringe/bangs and a strong parting. Keep your layers long and soft. Keep the hair below the jawline and go for layers that graze your cheekbones. Avoid short blunt bangs and choppy layers.

Handbags - When it comes to handbags, it is all about the function: where you are going, what you need to carry, and how long you need to carry it. Are you going for a date night? Work? The gym? Shopping? A casual social? Special occasion? Or are you on holiday and going to the beach?

TASK - START TO DRESS FOR SUCCESS AND HAPPINESS

Now, I want you to go start dressing for the success and happiness you want without apology or explanation. How does this make you feel? See how people react and interact with you. Are there any changes to their behaviour towards you and how many compliments do you get? Note your findings in your journal.

Also, you can start to clear out your wardrobe and make way for all those dream items you are going to reward yourself with when you reach your goals. If you need some additional support go complete the Wardrobe Workout challenge with a complete wardrobe checklist in the resource area that comes with this book. You can find it at:

www.yvonnephillip.com/book

16 / WHAT'S YOUR PERSONAL SEASONAL COLOUR PALETTE

The power of colour is incredible. Colour can evoke emotions that are subconsciously in us and make us feel happy, sad, uplifted, calm, relaxed, passionate and everything in between. How are the colours you are wearing affecting your happiness? Are you always wearing black and other dark colours, trying to hide away and sink into the background?

An understanding of the psychology of colour will help not only your decision making on what to wear, but also how to communicate your brand and create happiness through colour. We can do this either through the colours that suit you, as determined by your hair, eye, and skin tone, or the colours that suit your personality and the message you want to send. Both ways of looking at colour refer to the seasons, which is one of the simplest ways to understand colour theory. These methods do not relate to the season you were born but the visual and emotional connection it has.

Wearing the right colours can:

- Enhance your natural skin tone.

- Make you look younger.
- Lift your natural features.
- Make your skin look cleaner and healthier.
- Make your eyes appear brighter.
- Make your face look more defined.

Wearing less flattering colours can:

- Make you look tired and older.
- Cast shadows.
- Emphasis facial lines, wrinkles, and blemishes.
- Create an ashy or pasty complexion.
- Make your face look larger / fuller.
- Make your eyes look dull

YOUR PERSONAL COLOUR PALETTE

Let's first assess what colours best suit you and what seasonal palette you personally fit into. This is more about what colours are more flattering for you to wear to represent you in the right light and increase your personal impact and happiness. This will present you authentically and also send out the correct messages about you. We then need to take a deeper assessment into what seasonal palette that your brand personality fits into.

To determine your seasonal palette, you will first need to decide if you have a neutral, warm or cool skin tone.

- Warm Skin Tone - has peachy, yellow, or golden undertones.
- Cool Skin Tone - pink, red, or blue undertones.
- Neutral Skin Tone - a mixture of both.

Once you have established your skin tone, you need to take into account your eye and hair colours to see if they are light, bright, soft, or deep. The combination will allow you to determine your seasonal palette.

The first place to start is with your neutral colours, which will act as your wardrobe staples and building blocks of each and every outfit. Neutrals once again fit into cool and warm tones. Finding your tone is based on your skin undertones, as detailed above:

With warm neutral undertones, the colours that will suit you best are:

- Chocolate Brown
- Brown
- Rust
- Cream
- Camel
- Teal
- Olive green
- Tomato Red

With cool neutral undertones, the colours that will suit you best are:

- Black
- Grey
- White
- Navy
- Taupe
- Burgundy
- Pine Green

- Cherry Red

Finding the neutral colours that best suit you are a great way of starting a capsule wardrobe for yourself. Using your neutrals to mix with a small selection of colours will keep you on brand and receiving compliments throughout the day. In terms of finding those pops of colour, this is where your personal seasonal colours come into play.

TASK

Use the information below to identify what season your personal colourings fall into. If you cannot identify yourself, please reach out to me:

SPRING - WARM, CLEAR AND LIGHT

If you are a Spring, you have warm skin with bright and light features:

Hair Colour

- Golden blonde
- Light red or strawberry blonde
- Light to medium golden brown
- Light to dark golden-brown hair
- Coppery to red

Skin Colour

- Pale with peach or pink undertones
- Ivory to warm beige with pink undertone
- Warm brown, bronze, and dark brown
- Ivory, warm beige, bronze and might have freckles
- Eye Colour
- Blue, hazel, green or light brown

SUMMER - COOL, SOFT AND LIGHT

If you are a summer, you have cool skin with muted, blended features:

Hair Colour

- Platinum blonde/Ash blonde
- Blonde, brown / Light brown
- Brown grey (muted tone)
- Brown with auburn
- Blue grey

Skin Colour

- Peaches, creamy
- Beige/ lily with pink cheeks
- Beige/lily with no colour
- Pink beige
- Rose or charcoal-coloured freckles

Eye Colour

- Cloudy/grey blue
- Pale grey green/Pale grey

- Green (with white flecks)
- Blue (with white flecks)
- Hazel or soft brown

AUTUMN - WARM, SOFT AND DEEP

If you are an autumn, you have warm skin with muted blended features:

Hair Colour

- Red
- Copper (dark, red, brown)
- Chestnut (light red brown)
- Golden brown
- Charcoal black
- Golden grey

Skin Colour

- Ivory with golden freckles
- Golden beige (sallow)
- Peach with golden brown freckles
- Dark coppery beige
- Black with a golden undertone

Eye Colour

- Dark brown / Golden brown
- Amber / Hazel (golden, green, brown)
- Green (with brown or gold flecks)

WINTER - COOL, BRIGHT, AND DEEP.

If you are a winter, you have cool skin with bright prominent features:

Hair Colour

- Blue / black
- Medium brown (reddish highlights)
- Dark brown (grey beige tone)
- Salt and pepper/Silver grey
- White blonde

Skin Colour

- Lily white/Silver white
- White with pink undertones
- Beige/Rose beige
- Olive
- Black with a blue undertone
- Charcoal freckles

Eye Colour

- Dark reddish brown/Hazel
- Grey blue/Dark blue
- Blue with white flecks
- Grey green

17 / SEASONAL PERSONALITIES FOR BRANDS

In addition to which seasonal palette you personally fit into in terms of the colours that suit you, as a personal brand, we could also look at the seasons that suit your brand personality. These may be the same or they may be different.

Each season and style has a personality which you can use when selecting branding elements - we shall go into this later on. To ensure you have a cohesive brand, you must select one prominent season which should be based on colour. You can also select one subordinate season, at the most, which your other branding elements could come from.

There are positive and negative effects to each season. If you stick to one season, you will communicate all the positives in it and this in turn will communicate the personality of the brand and person behind it.

TASK

Go take the Brand Personality Quiz to find out your seasonal personality and the elements that suit each. You can find it at www.yvonnephillip.com/book

REFLECTION

1. Does your personal colour palette match your brand personality?
2. What season best matches the personality and archetypes you want for your brand?

Now that you have established the seasonal palettes that best suit your personal colouring and understand the personalities of each season, you can find the colours that best suit your brand. Colours that you can wear and colours that can be in your visual branding, if you decide that this is something that you would like to do.

It's ok if you find you or your business fit into one clear season, though this is rare. You, as a business of one, are unique and you may find you fall across more than one season. As mentioned before, you can have a dominant season and a subordinate season.

The dominant season will determine the tones of the colours you use. Do not use tones from different seasons as this will come across as confusing, make you look a hot mess and create the wrong emotional reaction. When you have decided on your dominant season, you can then take the elements (fonts, textures, patterns etc) from the subordinate season to fully create the essence of your brand, personal impact and who you are.

Now, the colours you use in your brand will represent the different values you or your business hold. With this in mind, it is important for us to identify which colours will communicate your core messages and feelings and select a palette that reflects your brand authentically.

TASK: COMPLETING YOUR WARDROBE WORKOUT

Once you have the key colours that are going to present you and the message you want to send, go back to the Wardrobe Workout that you may have already started and complete the task. This time go through and remove the colours and prints that don't suit your personality or your personal colour palette. Now, I want to be clear: when I say remove, I do not mean throw away. I want you to think about sustainability.

You can find the Wardrobe Workout challenge in the free resources that accompany this book. The key objective is to clear the clutter and identify what is required.

Visit www.yvonnephillip.com/book for the information.

18 / DEVELOPING YOUR
SENSE OF STYLE

Some people are lucky enough that they were born with a sense of style, others need a little support. I am not sure if I was born with it, all I know is style was always around me, from my Mum being a dressmaker to my Aunty being a Fashion and Textile Designer. I was always being used as a human dress dummy as they draped and pinned fabric over me. I was always flicking through the dress patterns and magazines for style inspiration and learnt from an early age how to put an outfit together.

I have never really put much into thinking about age, but in my forties, I got myself into a real style rut and decided that I needed to take a serious look at myself. This reignited my interest in becoming a style and image consultant.

I mentioned earlier that becoming a personal stylist was a life-long passion of mine, fulfilled as part of my 'Go Happy Yourself' journey. I was not showing up for myself. Every morning, I hauled myself out of bed, showered, looked in my wardrobe and said, 'I have nothing to wear'. I would open the second and then the third wardrobe door, all of which had rails and rails of clothes behind them, but still nothing. I had lost my style and needed to do something about it!

I decided to treat myself to a Personal Styling session with a local boutique that I liked. It was my birthday, and I had a fab time. As I was trying on the clothes, I began to remember that this was what I had wanted to do back in my early twenties. I wanted to be an image consultant. I even had the name - 'Images by Yves'. Unfortunately, I could not afford to train back then but I still have all the books I purchased instead of training on my shelf. A few days after my day at the boutique, I was looking for a 'Things to do' deal on a discount site when an offer came up to train to become a Personal Stylist. Not one to miss a bargain, I snapped it up straight away and the rest is history. I now focus on sustainable style as part of my wider offers, which include style power hours, remixing your wardrobe, personal brand shoots and videos together with my business and career strategy and selfcare services.

However, getting my sense of style back was not easy. As you know, looking young has been glorified as what you should always aim to achieve but my thing is, as long as you look and feel good, you should not need to be wrinkle free with no grey hairs at fifty. Although I think you should be able to dress how you want, you need to ensure that you dress appropriately for your age and activity. Not doing so can unfortunately attract the wrong type of attention and to people developing a misleading opinion of you. As we get older, we have to accept it and dress appropriately, in addition to dressing for the success and happiness you want and personality you want to share.

Here is what Celebrity Stylist and Personal Stylist Coach Lauren Messiah and I think on the topic of dressing for your age:

STYLE FOR YOUR 20'S

In your twenties your body is probably at its best, so with confidence you can pull off anything. Try as many of the latest trends, change things up and experiment. Have fun until you find what is right for you as a signature style.

You probably cannot afford the more expensive brands and opt for cheap, fast fashion. Being young means anything looks expensive, despite how cheap they are. But you must think about sustainability.

STYLE FOR YOUR 30'S

Your thirties are when you traditionally find out who you are and your true calling in life. You should have a career, business, life-long friends and perhaps a relationship but does your style match this?

It is the time to start to invest in a few classic pieces and start to ditch the fast fashion that only lasts a season or gets miss-shaped after a few washes. You can save time and money in the long run by investing in timeless pieces you can wear every day and using accessories to bring out your uniqueness.

Make sure you have a few stand out dresses that you can pull out for those all imported occasions: weddings, cocktail parties, work events etc. However, in your thirties it is time to cover up a bit. Select one sexy part of your body to show off instead of baring it all.

STYLE FOR YOUR 40'S

In your forties, any areas of your life such as your home, family and career should be good, but often not your style. Life has taken over and your style has been forgotten. I wanted to be youthful and cool but the teenagers in my life were making it clear that I was not so should stop trying. I needed to strike a balance between how I felt and wearing what was appropriate. I did not want to look frumpy but also did not want to look like mutton dressed up as lamb. It was, however, the perfect time to embrace who I was, what I liked and what I wanted.

Stay true to who you are and what looks good on you and do not follow the trends of the 20 somethings, bloggers and what is cool on the street. In your forties, it is time to develop your style uniform, making it easy to dress and enhance with accessories. There is always room for costume jewellery but now it is time to invest in some real precious pieces in terms of metal and stones. As in your thirties, it is time to show a little less flesh. You do not want to look like a cougar. That hot body can come across as desperate, especially if you are single and showing too much off.

STYLE FOR YOUR 50'S

I remember when I hit my fifties, my emotions and body went haywire as the menopause kicked in - what a pain! Hot flashes, or power surges as I like to call them. The redistribution of weight and unwanted hair making appearances are now the norm for most of us at this age. We all have to deal with it, so it is best to get ready to make the adjustments.

In addition to a good daily dose of supplements to support your regulation of balance and hormones. I want you to remember there is nothing wrong with being 50+, so don't try to dress as if you are 20 or 30. We need to be tasteful and timeless, with your growing collection of accessories such as scarves and bold earrings that will let your personality shine.

With your body thermostat doing its own thing, it is best to wear layers that way you can take off and put on clothes as your body demands. The final thing I think you should consider is your shoe game. Invest in quality and comfortable shoes and a statement handbag that will ensure you look and feel fab at all times.

STYLE FOR YOUR 60'S PLUS

It's strange that it was only when my grandmother and then my mother were in their 60s and 70s that I realised how absolutely hilarious they are. They tell it like it is and say what they want, and I believe this is how it should also be with your style.

At this age, you are wise enough and know yourself enough to wear whatever you want (within reason) and still look put together. You're also old enough to get away with whatever you want in terms of style and outfit creation. So have fun with bold colours and fabrics. It's time to get the luxury designer handbag, scarf, piece of jewellery, sunglasses or hat you have always had your eye on. You have earnt it!

Facts say that celebrities have a real impact on 48% of women's personal style, which is massive when you think about it because we trust celebrities more than we trust our friends - only 31% would ask their best friends for style advice. This would also explain why the magazines we read, and fashion brands feature celebrities so much. Where do you or could you get your style inspirations from?

- Style Icons
- Celebrities, films, TV shows
- Blogs and websites
- Magazines and online retailers

TASK - CREATING THE MOOD OF YOUR STYLE

Now is your time to get creative!

Create a mood board of inspirational photos of styles and items that you need and would like for your wardrobe collection. Use inspiration from magazines, websites, social media etc. You can create it in a scrapbook, on a cork board or you can use an app or software such as PicCollage or Pinterest which is my personal favourite.

You should now be clear on who you are and where you want to be through your style. Complete a style profile to ensure clarity by answering the following questions to yourself about your style:

1. What is the overall vibe of your new style?
2. What are the most important elements of your new style?
3. What's your seasonal colour palette?
4. Are there any accent colours you can use from the colours in your palette?
5. What is your body shape?
6. What silhouette and cuts should you be wearing?
7. What are the key fabrics and materials you like?

8. Are there any style techniques that stand out for your new look?

9. If your new style had a name, what would it be?

10. What is a typical outfit you would wear to work for your new style type?

11. What is a typical outfit you would wear out on a date for your new style type?

12. What is a typical outfit you would wear for the weekend for your new style type?

13. What does your new sense of style say about you?

14. What items do you already have that fit your new style type?

15. What pieces do you want /need to purchase to complete your new style?

19 / STRESSLESS SHOPPING

Shopping can be stressful if you shop to fill an emotional need, or if you 'shop till you drop', without a clear plan and end up overspending. It can also lead to stress if you do not do your research so do not find the best deals. It can be less stressful and bring more happiness if you are prepared and are aware of your body shape, seasonal colour palette and budget. It is also useful if you are aware of your style type, who inspires you and your dress code for success. In addition to the above, it is also good to get a clear idea on what shops stock the clothes that are right for you in terms of style and budget.

TASK

Put together a list of items you need for your wardrobe now and would like in the future. Remember, you need to dress for the success you want so it may be an idea to visit stores and brands outside of your budget and pop over to the sale section. Alternatively, you can gain inspiration then find similar looks elsewhere, such as preloved/vintage, swapping, renting, outlets and sustainable brands. When you try on your garments ask yourself:

1. Do I have something like this already?
2. Can I create at least 50 looks with this piece? (Think about your coats, bags, and accessories too)
3. Does it fit?
4. Can I afford it?
5. Can I re-sell or consign it later?
6. Why am I buying this?
7. What is my emotional state right now, is this an emotional purchase?

20 / SUSTAINABLE & ETHICAL STYLE

In addition to this, and as already mentioned, we need to consider sustainability. The fashion industry is the second most polluting sector globally. The first is oil! With this in mind, "Green is the new black!" and on the agenda are fashion brands from high street to high end.

I remember reading an article when I was at college where Stella McCartney championed the cause, way back in the late 1980s. More recently, she says her goal is to help consumers:

> 'To portray who we want to be and how we carry ourselves, our attitude and collective path. Our man-made constructed environments are disconnected and unaware of other life and the planet, which is why there is waste."

However, there are many different ways to look at the cause but to some, it's designing, sourcing, and manufacturing clothes in a way that benefits people and communities while minimising impact on the environment.

There are different ways to produce ethical fashion, and according to the Ethical Fashion Forum, they fall into three categories: social, environmental, and commercial, specifically tackling issues such as:

- Countering fast, cheap fashion and damaging patterns of fashion consumption.
- Defending fair wages, working conditions and workers' rights, and supporting sustainable livelihoods.
- Addressing toxic pesticide and chemical use, using and/or developing eco- friendly fabrics and components.
- Minimising water use.
- Recycling and addressing energy efficiency and waste.
- Developing or promoting sustainability standards for fashion.
- Providing resources, training and/or awareness raising initiatives.
- Protecting animal rights.

There are lots of brands that are focused on eco, fairtrade and sustainable style. I would not advise you to try to tackle all of the issues as it could become overwhelming, and some solutions affect others. I remember when I started my sustainable style journey, I thought I was going to have to walk around butt naked. So much information and actions conflicted with each other. But I found by deciding on a few - no more than 3 - sustainable style goals you want to support, you can map out your sustainable style path and new ways of shopping for good. Here are 10 simple ways you can shop more sustainably and ethically:

1. Shop in charity shops and thrift stores.
2. Rent items for that special occasion instead of buying them.
3. Have your go-to stores and check the brand's sustainability policy.
4. Establish what is important to you.
5. Mend items and give them a new lease of life.
6. Give old items to a charity shop or go have some fun at swapping events.
7. Consider if you can create at least 50 looks with this piece?
8. Consider if you can re-sell or consign it later?
9. Consider why you are buying this, is this an emotional purchase?
10. Would this add to the development of a capsule wardrobe?

REFLECTION

What are your sustainable style goals or which ones would you like to adopt? Mine is to reduce waste, fairtrade for workers and charitable giving. Do yours match your values in some way and how could you change the way you shop to support this?

21 / PUTTING YOUR STYLE
ALL TOGETHER

Research states that the average woman loses 17 minutes per day standing in front of her wardrobe / closet deciding what to wear each morning. This equates to around six months over the average lifetime. Just think about all the good things that you could do with six months extra time. Outfit planning can help this!

So, you have identified your style blocks, body shape, the colours that suit you, you have searched for inspiration and analysed your wardrobe against your lifestyle, may have been shopping and now we are coming to the end of the 'What you wear' part of the 'Go Happy Yourself' journey. You should have all the ingredients to claim that time back, relaunch yourself as the new stylish you.

TASK

Use your inspirational mood board and the current garments in your wardrobe /closet to put together at least 3 outfits that you feel will bring you the success you want. Ideally, you could plan for the month (30 outfits) but a week's worth of planning could be just as useful once you get used to it.

I don't want you to completely copy the outfits of someone you admire. I am sure you have experience of that purchase you make that looks amazing online or in the store then when you get it home and try it on it doesn't quite look the same. There are extra pits of fabric, the colour does not quite look the same and you are just not carrying it off. This could be because you are wearing someone else's style and not your own.

What I advise you to do is take what you like and use it to create your own unique style. You will also need to consider how you are going to pull your outfits together with your shoes, handbags, and jewellery, which will add the finishing touches and bring your outfits to the next level.

Now, get out there and introduce yourself to the world.

Merrisha Gordon is a Career Consultant and Coach and a client who works with public sector staff to elevate their careers and performance. I sat down with Merrisha to discuss the life-changing experiences she has been through and how owning her style has made her feel more confident.

Yvonne

Hi, Merrisha, thank you so much for joining me today as part of my book, and talking to me about the process that you've gone through to step up with clarity on who you are, and show up with more confidence. But before we get into all that good stuff, I just want you to give us a little bit of background about you, your career, and your upbringing.

Merrisha

I am working as an organisational consultant and a coach with the NHS in a corporate capacity, but I also work as a coach with female business owners. This represents a new chapter in my life. I've been working for myself for about seven months now, so it's still relatively new. This is on the back of saying farewell to a 21-year corporate career in the NHS. So, it's all very new, stepping outside of the job title, stepping outside of an organisation, and now standing on my own two feet and saying, "This is me, and I am the brand" - it's a very different space to be in. Not one that I thought I would be in, but I have to say, this is my 43rd year now and I have never felt happier, more vibrant, more confident, and energetic. I'm in an amazing place.

But it hasn't always been like that. I grew up in Birmingham on an inner-city council estate, so very much surrounded by all kinds of things ranging from mental health, poverty, and domestic violence - there were all kinds around me. I sought solace in books, so from a young age, I was always very academic, because that was my escape place. At the age of 11, I got into a quite prestigious secondary school, which was a good achievement. But at the same time, that was probably where some of my challenges started, because I was in this environment where I really didn't fit in. And the feeling of not fitting in really stood with me for a long time. So firstly, I was one of five black girls in my year and didn't really see people that looked like me, that were shaped like me, that spoke like me, I was mixing in very different circles. So, it didn't feel like I fit in at school. Most of my friends were white, which was fine, but I was regularly called duck. And the reason why I was called duck was because my bum stuck out, which, at the age of 11 is actually quite a pivotal time when your body starts changing. I hadn't realised it then, but I was curvy - I had hips, I had a bum, I had boobs, and my shame was very different to all of my friends. I hated it. I absolutely hated it.

Yvonne

Because they're making you feel not worthy. You're not good enough, you're different. With the colour of your skin blatantly saying that you're different. The fact that you don't have the same body shape and you feel that your body shape is not attractive. That would really play on your mindset.

Merrisha

Absolutely. I mean, people are paying thousands now for a bum, but back in the day they wouldn't! I couldn't get into my hockey skirt and that wasn't a good place for me. What made it even worse is that I wore these goddamn awful glasses, you know, milk bottle glasses. So, it was just not a great experience growing up as a teenager when it's already quite a vulnerable period of your life.

Yvonne

So, you've grown up very academic but feeling a little bit isolated. Obviously, you're going to school and you're not fitting in and then when you go home you've got a very different life-style to those other children at that prestigious school. So, there was an all-round mismatch. I mean, it helped you get your career and a well-paid job, etc., but did that feeling of not feeling worthy or not fitting in stick with you? Or were you able to shake that off when you went to university and entered the job market?

Merrisha

Do you know, I have to say it stayed with me for a long time and there was the massive imposter in me. I was the first person in my family to go to university and there was a lot of pressure put on me. Then I go to university and I'm suddenly with lots of international students who have travelled - people who have lived very different lives and have come from very different backgrounds. So, there was always that undercurrent of not feeling good enough. It didn't help that I just about passed my A-levels, because of course, once I came out of this prestigious school and went to college, that was a whole different chapter. So, I'd gone from being very academic and being focused, in an all-girl school to suddenly being in college and there were boys.

So suddenly, I realised curves were an attractive thing, because suddenly the boys were starting to notice. I had just scraped through and got into university by the skin of my teeth. So, there was a massive feeling of being an imposter. That's stayed with me for a heck of a long time. So, then I finished my studies, and I moved to London, started my job and I started my career as an administrator. Within a year, I was in my first NHS management position - which was fantastic. But at the time, I was 22 and managing staff who were the same age as my mom. I looked incredibly young and was surrounded by people who didn't look like me. I remember really dialling down and trying to fit in. I was really taking in how other people were dressing and trying to fit into what I saw was the mould of an NHS manager. I can remember working in a central London Hospital and spending an awful lot of money on Hobbs clothes - and it was fine. But at the age of 27-28, when I was buying in Hobbs, I had no business buying Hobbs. But I was surrounded by hospital consultants and surgeons and all these people that had very different backgrounds.

Yvonne

Different backgrounds and definitely a different stage in their life. You know, you were young, just starting your career - they were more established, and you wanted to fit in and assert yourself as a manager and as a leader. It wasn't you.

Merrisha

It wasn't me - for a long time. There were lots of things that were starting to align with me and starting to find me. I remember 7/7, and somebody I knew had unfortunately lost their life in 7/7. I remember being at this person's funeral and taking stock and thinking about the things that he wanted to do. I wanted to pierce my nose, and I wanted to grow locks. I'd always been told, "Oh, you can't have your hair like that - it's not corporate, you won't fit in, you won't get the jobs."

I came out of that funeral: I pierced my nose and I decided to grow locks. I had locks for about 16 years up until about 18 months ago. That was the start of me finding myself - but I still always felt like a bit of an outsider. People generally didn't realise this because I suppose I came across as confident. But for so many years, I was really trying to find out who I was and what I liked in every area of my life. This theme continued, and it probably started changing as I started down the psychology route, which was in my early 30s. It started with coach training: I was doing a master's in psychology to go down the path of retraining as a psychologist. There was something about being in those spaces and going through therapeutic training, where you suddenly start doing a lot of reflection, a lot of self-analysis. I became a lot more self-aware, and really started to ask myself different questions, but I'd not always been brave enough to follow the answers.

Yvonne

Absolutely and this is what this book is all about. It's about asking those questions, so that the readers can actually find the answers for themselves. They can find the answers to create the happiness, the visibility, the success that they want. So, when did you decide that enough is enough? That you needed to step up as yourself and that there was no right or wrong time to do it, you just had to take the step forward?

Merrisha

Hitting 40 was a big thing for me. It made me take stock with - Who am I? Where am I going? Am I happy? Am I living my life the way that I want to live it? At that point, I had a baby and for my 40th birthday, I'd gone on this girly weekend to Dubai - I left the baby at home and just buggered off. That was the start of me really starting to find myself again. That was also tied in with doing some NLP training, which was completely transformative. Because I then had nowhere to hide. I couldn't hide from these questions that kept coming up.

So, I made some massive life changes. I was in an unhappy relationship, and I decided I'd had enough. So, I left my daughter's dad when she was 18 months old. It was quite a traumatic breakup, but actually, you have to have that breakdown before you get your breakthrough. And that was when I absolutely realised the strength and the power that lay within. This all happened just before the pandemic. I became a single parent and all of a sudden, my financial situation had changed overnight. I had a mortgage: the nursery fees were more than the mortgage and suddenly things got real. I had to do different things. I remembered I had this coaching qualification that I wasn't using, so I started doing more coaching. As I started doing more coaching - and as I had the freedom from not having the backdrop of an unhappy relationship - I started finding the answers. Ironically, that's also when my style changed.

Yvonne

You said to me, that you felt like you'd lost your style and that working on your style has actually made you feel like you again which was absolutely beautiful. So, tell us about that loss of style.

Merrisha

I think it was definitely having a baby and being in an unhappy relationship. I was breastfeeding for 16 months - 16 months too long. Everything became very practical. But it also reflected the fact that I was just in a miserable place. It's only when I look back now, and I see photos where I barely smile, and everything I wore was black and navy.

Yvonne

That's not what we see now.

Merrisha

If I ever put on anything black, it's got something bright over it. Otherwise, I can't wear it. Because it just doesn't feel like me to be in black or navy. It's not me. I lived in black and navy. I guess I was trying to hide and trying to blend in. Psychologically, I was trying to hide. This body was a different body to the one that I'd had, and I didn't really know what to do with it.

Yvonne

All those baby changes and the emotions that that brings up. How you're feeling also towards your ex-husband or partner as well. Your whole psyche had changed at that moment. When you're growing up, you hear about your life going in seven-year blocks, but you don't think about it as if it really happens like that.

Merrisha

Yeah, it absolutely did. I just kind of got in this space where I was doing lots of coaching and I was trying to make an effort with my style even though I wasn't going very far, because I recognised that it was really good for my mental health. But I would have peaks and troughs. I even recognised. once I started working for myself, that the only place I was going was the school run. I started to feel a little bit flat. I was loving what I was doing in terms of work, but I wasn't really connecting with people. I wasn't really going anywhere, and I was just getting back into comfortable clothes again.

Yvonne

Well, absolutely, we all have had that little spread that we get when we're not moving too far over the last few years - that's the world that we've been living in. So, you don't actually show up as yourself because people only need to see from your chest upwards. But in doing that, whether it's in a pandemic or not, it's just gonna make you feel unworthy, and your self-esteem is gonna go down. Then you're going to just want to hide. So, when did you realise that you needed to start showing up with a little bit more confidence and your style could possibly be the thing that helps you do that? Because I know you're not shy of taking photos.

Merrisha

No, I'm not. It's interesting because I had a brand shoot last year to start putting myself out there on social media and my website. One thing I do like now is colour. So, I've got all these things that were colourful, but I looked at the pictures and it still did not feel like me. What I realised is I was spending a lot of time looking online at what other people were doing for their websites and how they were dressing and almost got myself into a spin where I'd bought these clothes that I thought I should be wearing as a coach.

Yvonne

I remember when I saw your original brand photos. I was like, these are beautiful dresses, but that's not the vibe I get from Merrisha from initial impressions. Then I saw you at a Christmas party and I saw something completely different.

Merrisha

Something in me told me that I needed pastel and frilly, and I don't know where it came from.

Yvonne

But you know what? That's right for somebody, but that wasn't right for you and your brand.

How did you find what was right for your brand? What was the process and when did you realise you need to start dressing for you body shape right now and not for your body shape that you want. The number of women that I work with who want to lose weight, but they know that if they wait until they lose weight, they're just gonna be still stuck in the rut. So, let us make the change for what I'm like now, and at least I've got something to work for. But at least I am looking fabulous while I'm working towards it.

Merrisha

And that is the thing because I can tell you, I'm the heaviest I've been for a long time at the moment. But I'm feeling fabulous. Where that has come from is about connecting with my authentic self. What is my brand about? My brand is about colour. Colour is really important to me, because it's vibrancy, it's joy, it exudes happiness, it's energy, and these are all the things that are authentic to me and that's what I bring to my coaching. If you were to ask me about my values, then it is about authenticity. It is about being me. It is about not trying to be a carbon copy of someone else. It is about recognising - yes, I am a coach and I've got all of these qualifications, but actually, I'm a pie and mash girl from a council estate in Birmingham. I don't want to lose that by trying to pretend to be somebody else. It is really important that I feel like myself.

Yvonne

Absolutely. So how does this transcend into your style? You mentioned prior that you had a brand shoot, and you wore all these pastel frilly colours. You were thinking about, "I need to be like everybody else." Now it's been reversed to "I need to show up as who I am, as my authentic self." What was that feeling? What type of feeling did you get when you actually looked at yourself in the mirror, and you were styled in your new brand style that you've created for yourself with a little bit of guidance.

Merrisha

I'd put on the clothes and I was feeling like hot stuff. I wasn't wearing anything particularly special - I wasn't wearing body con or anything like that. But I really felt hot because the clothes complimented me, they fit me nicely, the colours were me and I said, "I feel like me." Which was really, really important to me.

Yvonne

Have you ever been fearful of taking photos? Did the fact that you felt fabulous add to that confidence or were you already okay with taking photographs?

Merrisha

People think I'm a natural and I love taking pictures, but I can be really quite highly critical of myself. I will take the pictures and then I look at them and pick out all the ones I hate - that has always been the theme. So, to get to a place where I haven't even seen the pictures, but just know they're going to be absolutely amazing is also absolutely amazing.

Yvonne

It's great when you haven't even seen what the photographer was doing but you knew they were going to be great.

Merrisha

They're going to be great - because I felt great. What is in here, came out. I am confident that there was a level of congruence going on that day. What I felt was coming out.

Yvonne

What do you think, in addition to the outfits that you were wearing and the beautiful location, added to that sense of confidence or happiness when you had the brand shoot experience?

Merrisha

It was everything. I found the process of the questionnaire, then the styling session review and trying on the clothes - I found that absolutely amazing. I didn't realise that's how we were going to do it. But actually, it was so powerful, because there is this critical eye. But you do it with love. I know you're not gonna let me fail and that was really reassuring. But the thought process before we even started trying on the clothes, made me really think about what it is that I wanted to project on the day.

Yvonne

At the end of the day, that's what you wanted to be at the photoshoot - feeling like a million bucks. That's the feeling that we want to get, and I want that feeling for women every day.

Merrisha

Yeah. And that's how I felt. You know, when you're trying on something new, and you look in the mirror and you think, "Oh, I don't want to take this off." That is how I felt. Then you've got this amazing makeup artist who just got it, you know, I didn't have to sit there and explain anything, she just got it. She was fantastic. In this fantastic location, with this fantastic group of women who were there to cheer each other on - it was just magical.

Yvonne

I just kept on hearing laughter - and that was great because that proved to me that coming together as a group to do these things, as women, as entrepreneurs with a common goal and a common purpose was so powerful. We've been in lockdown and as entrepreneurs, we spend a lot of time on our own, especially as online entrepreneurs.

So, we don't know what these photos look like yet, but we know in ourselves that they're going to be amazing. And I've noticed that you've already used a snapshot of yourself on set in your social media. How else are you going to use this newfound confidence to grow your business?

Merrisha

So, it's really interesting because there has been an undercurrent around visibility for a while. I've been having conversations with people virtually, it's all fine. But there was this fear about going live. There's this fear around how I show up on social media. I'm not hiding behind the day job now, this is me. I did an Instagram Live on Sunday for the first time, and I don't know what came over me. I just still had that energy with me and I just thought "you know what, get over yourself girl. You have got things to talk about." So, I did! I did an Instagram Live, I thought I'd be on there for a few minutes. I was on there for 23 minutes,

Yvonne

You see! You've got lots of sharing to do. Now you need to make sure you stay consistent. Think about what you're going to say, don't let it be a burden on you.

Merrisha

I'm not trying to fit into somebody else's cookie cutter mould of what an online coach or an online business should be because it just feels a bit icky. So, what I am now recognising is that it's about what feels comfortable and authentic to me.

Yvonne

Yes, it's about what makes you happy. If it doesn't feel right for you then you need to change things up. Yes, we need a strategy, but we need a strategy that works for you and the way you communicate.

Merrisha

Absolutely. That energy has definitely stayed with me. I have also realised that I have been doing my makeup properly since that day. All the stuff I used to do before I had a child! There was something about getting my makeup done and connecting to the things I used to do before becoming a mum. I am feeling really good.

Yvonne

You are happy in yourself. Happiness transcends through the camera lens and if we want to get visible then the camera is the ideal place to do it. What is next for Merrisha and her visibility now?

Merrisha

I am really working on my visibility now. I have recently developed a 3-month program for women that I cannot wait to get started on. A lot of love, care and kindness has gone into creating this. But it requires being visible and getting out there so people can see why they should work with me. What I really want to do is to connect with people. I am also still coaching and training in the corporate space, but I don't want to be stuck in corporate. I want to be working with people who have been just like me.

Yvonne

You have gone through this transition, what advice would you give to any woman who wants to step out of her comfort zone and get some visibility and happiness into their lives?

Merrisha

One of the things I would always say to do is to get out of your head, connect with your heart and follow your guts. If I had stayed in my head, the single mother in me with a mortgage would have said "don't quit that job with the sick pay and the pension and all that security" and I would have been in that job till I was 65. But it didn't sit right with me in my heart and my soul. It wasn't making me happy, and I knew my passion lay in coaching and supporting others. So, I did what I tell all my clients to do and I followed my heart. Yes, there are practical elements like finances, but when you find something that you are good at and that is your passion, and you follow that, then it will work itself out.

Yvonne

The world is your oyster when you do what is true to you and when you follow your happiness. Think about having an impact on others rather than personal gain.

Merrisha

Absolutely - and also to connect with your 'why'. Why are you doing what you're doing? If you are driven by money, then that may work in the short term but long term, that is not going to make you happy.

Yvonne

Most definitely.

23 / YOUR VOCAL
BUSINESS CARD /
ELEVATOR PITCH

One of the key skills you need to master as an employee or entrepreneur is networking. An elevator pitch or vocal business card helps you with this. An elevator pitch is a brief, persuasive speech that you use to generate interest in what you do. You can also use them to create interest in a project, idea, product or in yourself. A good elevator pitch should last no longer than a short elevator ride of 20 to 30 seconds, hence the name.

We will tackle networking later. First, you need to craft these all-important 4 or 5 sentences so that you can create the best first impression and action you require.

You can use your mission statement as your elevator pitch, but this is a very general, high-level overview that will probably be too long for this purpose. It is, however, a great way to start a conversation if you are unsure of what part of your product or service may be appropriate for the person you are speaking to.

In this section, we are going to go through two different ways to provide an elevator pitch, you can select which one is best for you or adapt them as you see fit.

ELEVATOR 1 - This is good if you are looking for work or running a business. It is structured in 4 or 5 parts:

Introduction - Introduce yourself and what you do:

I.E: *"My name is Yvonne Phillip, and I am a Holistic Success and Visibility Consultant"*

You may want to pause here to ask the person's name and shake hands.

What You Do - Tell them what you do or what you can do for them:

I.E: *"I help female employees and entrepreneurs to elevate their personal brands through 1:1 services, online training and in-person experiences which provide a step-by-step system to success and visibility, either through career or business development, self-branding techniques or branding assets."*

Proof of Value - Provide evidence that you can do what you say you can do:

I.E: *"I have over 25 years' experience. I have supported over 500 people into employment and 150 to get job promotions. I am currently working with a number of female entrepreneurs, supporting them to consolidate and accelerate their brand message, both in person and online, through personal styling, photo and video shoots."*

Investigate needs (optional) - So that you can tailor your call to action, you may want to insert a question here:

I.E: *"How do you feel your personal brand is being represented currently?"*

They will provide you with information that will influence how you move forward.

Call to Action - Ask for what you want and be specific. This could be learning more about the company, exchanging contact details, having a coffee, work shadowing, an introduction to someone else etc.

I.E: *"I would love to share some tips on effective holistic personal branding with you and others, do you feel this would be useful?"* Or

"I would love to find out more about ...(what you would like to find out more about) would you be interested in discussing this further?"

ELEVATOR 2 - The second option is great if you are a coach, mentor, therapist etc.

Not a lot of people understand transformational methods and modalities like coaching and healing and if people don't understand what you do, they will not be willing to buy your products or services!

Here is a powerful, effective way to do this. There are two parts to this process. Firstly you'll need to create a powerful, client-attracting name for your offer, and then you'll put it in your perfect elevator pitch. This formula is great for attracting high-paying clients because people invest in you based on emotion and results:

I'm (your name), *creator of* (your Signature System name) *that helps* (the type of people or businesses) *who* (experience the pain or problem) *to get* (your powerful result).

When you use an elevator speech in this format with people at a networking event, they will know exactly who to refer you to, and whether they themselves are ideal clients or employers. You also sound like an authority, so it's easier to attract people who are willing to invest at a high level for the particular transformation that you provide.

One of the keys to having people eager to work with you is to include the name of your Signature System in your elevator speech. Your Signature System has to be named to reflect the transformation that you provide, so the client is really clear what they'll get out of it.

TASK

Quickly draft the contents of your elevator pitch in your journal.

Telling stories is a great way to build rapport, connection and trust with potential clients, employers or business partners. As customers often make decisions and buy on emotion, not logic, you need to build a relationship with them so they know you understand their struggle and can help them make the transformation they want.

Stories can be used when face to face in presentations, pitches and when networking. They can also be used online in social media posts, videos and blogs etc. You may have a number of stories that you can tell. What will your story/stories be?

While telling your story it may be useful to use the hero's journey as a template or following structure taken from Donald Miller's Story Brand:

- You can relate to the situation. You want to start with facts on the issue or pain point and how you and others can relate to it.

- You have struggled too. Build an emotional connection by talking about the what, when, where, why and how you went through in relation to the situation.
- You found a new way of doing things and it worked. Detail your light bulb moment, what you did about it, and any support you had. What product or service have you developed as a result of this.
- You found a new way of doing things that worked for others. Use testimonials and quotes from people that have used your products or service to prove that it works.
- They can try it too! Let them know how they can have the same results and how. Detail here your call to action and create urgency with a time limitation if relevant.

Write out these key elements and then add more emotion to the story with details! For job interviews, you can also use the STAR model to share stories, situations and examples of when you have used, gained or experienced what the interviewer is questioning you about.

The STAR module works as follows:

S - Situation. Set the scene for the story, by sharing context around the situation or challenge you faced. Share any relevant details.

T - Task. What was your role? Describe your responsibility or role in the situation or challenge.

A - Acton. What did you do? Explain how you handled the situation or overcame the challenges. If the action was taken by a team, focus on your part.

R - Result. How did the situation end? What was the outcome because of your actions? Qualify your success with examples.

To get yourself started, you may want to take some time to spend reflecting and writing a chronological timeline of your life story. Once you have done this, you can select different stores for different situations that you want to tell. You don't have to tell all of your whole life story, just the elements that you feel safe and confident to do so. However, a full life story could be a great download from the 'About Me' page on your website if you decide to have one.

TASK - STORY OUTLINE

It is great to have a bank of stories ready to go, so take 5 minutes to outline some of your stories with keywords only. Use the points above to outline at least one of your stories using either of the outlines above. When you have detailed your outline, you can develop on this as and when needed.

Remember, facts tell, and stories sell. Backup your story or start it with some facts, figures and rational arguments to reinforce what you are saying and illustrate your talents, skills and experiences in an authentic way. It is also important that the facts about you stand up to scrutiny when under questioning.

In some stories, it is great to mention what you are working on right now. This shows you are in demand. Beware, however, not to appear too busy as they may feel you will not have time for them.

So, by now you should be clear on the archetype(s) that you are going to evoke consistently in particular situations. Using words that strengthen your archetype within your brand creates a more powerful message. Here are a few words that you may want to use for each:

The Caregiver: Care, Altruism, Helper, Saint, Protect, Comfort, Nurture, Parent, Helper, Supporter, Affection, Empathy, Commitment, Friendly, Concern.

The Creator: Create, Innovative, Self-expression, Non-conformist, Vision, Invent, Inspiration, Daydreamer, Fantasy, Decoration, Experiment, Unconventional, Beauty, Aesthetic.

The Explorer: Discover, Seek, Wander, Find Out, Adventure, Individual, Pioneer, Freedom, Risk, Fearless, Curious, Explore, Experience, Restless.

The Hero: Courage, Proving your worth, Challenge, Competition, Strong, Powerful, Determination, Preserve, Prevail, Rescue, Discipline, Character, Warrior, Turnaround.

The Innocent: Purity, Goodness, Happiness, Simplicity, Paradise, Trusting, Honesty, Idyllic, Childlike, Rebirth, Perfectionist, Stress-reducing, Romantic, Naive Mystic.

The Jester: Live for the moment, Breaking the rules, Impulsive, Joker, Trickster, Prankster, Clown, Entertainer, Fool, Mischievous, Manipulative, Playful, Light-hearted, Outrageous, Clever.

The Lover: Partner, Intimate, Harmony, Sensory, Pleasure, Intimacy, Beautiful, Romance, Relationship, Attractive, Passion, Erotic, Gratitude, Appreciation, Commitment, Friendship.

The Magician: Realise a vision, Transform, Change, Spiritual, Mediator, Finds win-win solutions, Makes dreams come true, Charisma, Flow and Miracles.

The Ordinary Guy / Girl: Connect, Belong, Friend, The boy or girl next door, Good neighbour, Down to earth, Humanitarian, Functional, Straightforward, Wholesome, Realist, Team Spirit, Unpretentious.

The Outlaw: Breaks the rules, Revolutionary, Rebel, Disrupt, destroy, Outrageous, Radical, Counterculture, Unacceptable, Unconventional, Outsider, Independent thinking.

The Ruler: Boss, Control, Order, Commanding, Authority, Power, Substance, Impressive, Organiser, Responsible, Manager, Administrator, Dominator, Royalty.

The Sage: Scholar, Knowledge, Wisdom, Truth, Objectivity, Expert, Adviser, Mentor, Teacher, Research, Detect, Think, Interpret, Understand.

A metaphor is a figure of speech in which a word or phrase is applied to an object or action but is not literally or factual true. For example, when we talk about time or money you may hear people use the following metaphors: "Time is money", "Living on borrowed time", "Time is running out", "Money does not grow on trees," "Robbing Peter to pay Paul," "Money is the root of all evil."

Using metaphors can be useful in expressing your brand – as long as they are not overused so that they become cliches. This is particularly the case if used in written material. Use metaphors but use them sparingly, if you are clear on your archetype, you can use one that works well for example:

- A Hero may: Fight for survival
- A Ruler may: Strengthen the foundations
- A Creator may: Build a platform for growth

REFLECTION

How can you use your story or storytelling to enhance your prospect of happiness? Take one of your story outlines and flesh it out using key facts, words and maybe a metaphor or two that will truly bring your brand to life.

25 / YOUR BIOGRAPHY

A personal biography(bio) is a great way to express to people who you are and what you do. Whether your bio is for a college/university application, a professional website, a social media account, or the "about me" page, take your time and be thoughtful about what you write so you get the right message across.

Aim for at least 250 words for your website "about me" if you decide having a website would be good for you and what you want to do to create your happiness. This is just enough to give the reader a taste of your life and personality without them getting bored. Avoid a profile that is longer than 500 words. For social media this may be a lot shorter.

Here is a 10 point checklist to help you produce your bio:

1. Your purpose and audience. Your bio is your first introduction to your audience so before you start writing, think about your audience. Adjust your tone to make your bio appropriately formal, funny, professional, or personal.

2. Look at examples directed toward your target audience. One of the best ways to understand what your audience will expect from your bio is to look at the bios others in your field have written. See how they present themselves and figure out what you think they do well. Good places to look for professional bios could be professional websites and LinkedIn pages.

3. Narrow down your information. Keep your details relevant and informative. Your credibility is important here. For example, an author's bio on a book jacket often mentions past writing accomplishments, whereas an athlete's bio on a team website often mentions the person's height and weight. Make sure the info you give is relevant.

4. Write in the third or first person. Writing in the third person will make your bio sound more objective, as if it has been written by another person. Writing in the first person is more personal and approachable. It is up to you to decide which way is best for which platform and use.

5. Begin with your name. Assume that the people reading the bio know nothing about you and start with your preferred name.

6. State your claim to fame. What are you known for? What do you do for a living? How much experience or expertise do you have? Don't leave this to the end or make your readers guess—they won't, and they may well lose interest if this information is not given up front.

7. Mention your most important accomplishments, if applicable. If you have earned achievements or awards that are relevant, include them. But remember that a

bio is not a cv/resume. Do not simply list your accomplishments; describe them. Remember that your audience may have no idea who you are, so tell them.

8. Include personal, humanising details. Invite the reader to care about you by adding in personal facts at the end to balance out the professional. This is a chance to get some of your personality across. Avoid too much self-deprecation or being too intimate. These personal details will serve as conversation-starters should you meet your audience in real life.

9. Conclude by including information on any projects you have in the works. For example, if you're a writer, state the title of the new book you're working on. This should be kept to a sentence or two.

10. Include contact information. This is usually done in the last sentence. If it's to be published online, be careful with the email address in order to avoid spam. Many people write email addresses online as something like: Sarah (at) happymail (dot) com. Include other ways to contact you, such as via your social media profiles.

TASK

Look at examples of bios directed toward your target audience. One of the best ways to understand what your audience will expect from your bio is to look at the bios others in your field have. Once you have done your research, start to draft your bio using the format provided.

YVONNE PHILLIP

26 / SPEAKING AND
PRESENTING

Giving presentations is part of growing in your career and business. It's a valuable life skill to have as it can often be part of an interview process, sales process, to persuade your boss that you deserve a pay rise, deliver training or even to get your ideas and concepts across.

However, delivering a presentation is daunting and can bring up nerves and anxiety. Let's take some time to understand how effective presentations are structured so you can present in a more confident and relaxed manner.

A great presentation will make you feel either inspired, educated or informed about the topic. This is because presentations are structured in a logical and easy way for the audience to follow and take away key messages. Structured information is 40% more accurately remembered by audiences than unstructured information research shows. It will also help you as the presenter to stay on topic, avoid any awkward pauses as well as stay calm.

Any good presentation will have a natural flow to it, however not all presentations are structured the same. This will be due to a number of reasons, including:

- If demonstrations are included in the delivery.
- What knowledge the audience already has on the topic.
- What and how much audience interaction you want to include.
- The length of your talk.
- What location or setting you are in.
- The visual aids you use.

Before choosing the presentation's structure, answer these questions first:

1. What is the aim of your presentation's?
2. Who is the audience?
3. What main points do you want people to remember, take away and take action on?

Below is the usual structure of a presentation and is a good starting point for yours whether it be a presentation to selling a solution, persuade or problem solve:

1. Greet the audience and introduce yourself

You need to introduce yourself and your relevant expertise. This starts to build a relationship and trust with the listeners.

2. Introduction

The introduction needs to grab the audience's attention and connect with them. Explain the topic and purpose of your presentation to grab the listeners interest in what you are about to say. This can include issues or challenges you will explore and how you will address this i.e. "I will argue that..." or "compare", "analyse", "evaluate", "describe" etc.

You will also need to let the listener know what you hope the outcome will be and the length of the presentation. When questions will be taken and if they should take notes or if handouts / copies of the slides will be provided.

3. The main body of your talk

The main body part of your presentation needs to expand on the points described in your introduction. You will need to separate the different topics and then work through them one at a time. Separating them by theme, chronologically or priority so that they are organised logically and the audience fully understands and can follow. After each point, you should provide a mini conclusion that links to the next point or idea.

4. Conclusion

Your conclusion should reinforce your messages, goals and themes created in the main part of your presentation so that the purpose is reinforced. You can do this by signalling you are coming to the end by saying something like "I would like to conclude by...". You will then need to summarise the main points, implications and conclusions followed by the call to action or thought you would like them to take away.

5. Thank the audience and invite questions

Some presenters like to take questions as part of the presentation, I personally like to take them at the end. This allows you to focus on the content of the talk without distraction, you will also find that most points are answered in later presentation content so it reduces the number of questions.

TASK – PREPARE YOUR TALK / PRESENTATION / PITCH

Use the information above to start to prepare a presentation. The theme of the presentation can be anything that will help you get what you want as part of your 'Go Happy Yourself' journey

There are also other things you will need to consider when presenting, these include:

- Physical movement and slides
- Body Language
- Delivery
- Your voice
- Audience relations
- Overcoming fears

Let's go through each of these individually.

PHYSICAL MOVEMENT AND SLIDES

Moving your location on stage or in the room as you transition to another point or slide helps the audience to follow your presentation and could increase engagement.

Slides can be powerful in communicating your message. However, there are some presenters who choose not to use slides at all. Slides can be a powerful tool. If used properly, they can greatly assist in the delivery of your message and help the audience follow along with what you are saying. Key slides include:

- An intro slide outlining your ideas.
- High quality images or graphic slides to support what you are saying.
- A summary slide with core points to remember.

Your slides are there to assist your key points, do not overfill them. Instead use an image or diagrams to support what you are saying. Make sure any text is readable from the back of the room and do not rush, give people time to take in the information.

Guy Kawasaki, an entrepreneur and author, suggests that slideshows should follow a 10-20-30 rule:

- There should be a maximum of 10 slides – this will ensure people don't get overwhelmed with information.
- Your presentation should last no longer than 20 minutes, (there is a reason Ted Talks are only 18 minutes long) this will leave time for questions and discussion.
- The font size should be a minimum of 30 pt so ensure the audience can not only read the information but are less likely to get distracted.

BODY LANGUAGE

Consider your body language and the message that it conveys. Stand in a relaxed upright position with your hands by your side or in front of you. You can gesture to make a point but ensure this and your facial expressions are in line with the message you want to give.

DELIVERY

Delivery is everything when you are speaking, your points will get lost if your audience cannot follow you so; speak slowly and deliberately to the point when it seems too slow. Pause between ideas so your listener can digest the information. Do not mumble, make sure you articulate and pronounce your words and avoid words that you may trip over when speaking. Try to avoid filler words like Ah or Um, this comes from preparation and knowing your stuff. Add interest by varying the tone and pitch of your voice to keep the audience's interest and to draw focus to key points.

YOUR VOICE

Most people do not like the difference in a recording of the sound of their own voice. We sound different because people hear our voice through sound waves in the air and we hear our own voice through vibration in our skull. We sound harsher than we think and accents seem stronger. Accents add to your authenticity, so I would not advocate that you completely try to change how you speak, but ensure you are understood by others.

Diaphragmatic breathing is breathing from your diaphragm and not your chest and it can dramatically improve the quality of your voice. This is how professional singers breathe, it provides a richer tone that will help you to control your tone, pitch and the volume of your voice.

You can also use our voice to evoke our archetype, through pace and tone. A deeper tone adds authority, higher tones more questioning. For example, if your voice goes up at the end of a sentence it will sound like a question. If it goes down, it will sound like more of a command.

AUDIENCE RELATIONS

Being in tune with your audience is essential for speakers, it is more than standing in front or sitting and talking. You need to create an immediate connection and the best way to do this is through eye contact and talking as soon as you are introduced. Even if that means talking to them as you set up.

Make eye contact and smile and watch the audience. If they are smiling and nodding you are in a good place. If they look confused or distracted you need to adjust what you are saying or your delivery style.

OVERCOMING YOUR FEARS

As mentioned, anxiety and fears around speaking are natural, remember you are not the only one that feels this way about speaking publicly. Try to use the affirmations we created in pillar one to confirm how great you are and also the reframing technique available in the Mindset Makeover video available in the free resources that come along with this book. Although fears around public speaking is normal, if you have extreme fears about this or anything else it is important that you seek the support of a professional as this is going to hinder your happiness.

27 / PRESENCE AND CHARISMA

Charisma, like your personality, comes from within. It is like a magnet that attracts colleagues, clients, customers, investors, partners, friends and raving fans to you. This is essential when building a strong personal or business brand, but it needs to be authentic for you to create true happiness.

When a person has a strong presence, you feel it when they walk into a room. They often build rapport with others quickly and give every situation their complete undivided attention. They pay attention to what you do, say, think, and feel, and respond appropriately to create connections and trust. With the average person taking in information six times faster than they speak, we often think about how we are going to respond rather than actually listening to what the other person is saying. Technology does not help this and hinders our ability to communicate with others. Try not to check your mobile device or, even better, turn it off to ensure you are present.

Our next task will help you to focus your mind and be present. You may have to do it a few times but after a while start to use parts of the exercise when you are with people. You should find yourself listening to people and absorbing more information which will lead to you being able to build a stronger rapport with them. You can also use part of the exercise when you are speaking, maybe on stage or at a meeting. Feel your body as it moves, its weight on the floor to make sure you remain present.

TASK - BEING MINDFULLY PRESENT

Sit up straight and comfortably, close your eyes and make sure your feet are flat on the floor and your legs are uncrossed. Place your hands open on your thighs and relax your body.

Feel: the clothes touching your skin, your body on the chair and the air on your skin.

Listen: to the distant sounds and then bring your focus to the sounds nearby.

Taste: your mouth

Smell: the air, take a deep breath and let the air fill your lungs

Open your eyes and look at the colours and objects around you.

Rest here for a little while, feeling, listening, tasting and letting the smells and breath flow through your body.

Write in your journal. What do you notice?

We often go about our daily life feeling and thinking we are separate from everyone and everything. This is called duality. Whether at work, business, or in your personal life, if you see yourself as separate, you will not be able to connect with others and create happiness. For the businessperson, or those looking for work, this could come across and seem cold or desperate when trying to get a job, promotion, or new client.

When you interact with others you must create unity to help you build your brand and happiness. We are connected with everything and everyone on some level as what we say, do, and the way we act will have an effect, either positively or negatively. We have all heard the saying 'What goes around comes around', so serve others and you will serve yourself. Think about how you can be of service and connect to others on a deeper level to assist in the outcome you want.

Your mission for happiness involves using your talents to do what you love, in a way that matches your values. If you pursue your mission, you are likely to attract people to you due to your energy and enthusiasm in doing what you love. This authentic nature will attract the right people to you and the wrong people for you will stay away. By attracting the people that share some of your values and appreciate your talents, will ensure you are on a similar wavelength which makes your life, career, and business more productive and enjoyable.

Charisma can also come from accepting who you are and who other people are. People who accept themselves do not try to be anything they are not. They do not judge themselves or others and they show this through their body language, smile and style. Think about how you can improve your presence and charisma through eye contact, smiling, open body language, and genuinely matching others' positivity and moving away from negativity.

TASK

As you wake up each morning, I want you to say to yourself 'I shall accept everything that happens today'. Now, this may be difficult and you may not agree, but I want you to accept, register it and remain present. You will notice other people's behaviour and make judgments, that is natural. Let that judgement go and just accept it.

When you do this, it does not mean you do not care. It just means you can stay present and take action based on the here and now, and stay positive. If you feel negative feelings developing, take a deep breath, and feel your body until it returns to the present.

REFLECTION

Part 1: Check your behaviour towards other by answering the following questions about yourself:

- Are you approachable and friendly?
- Do you keep to your promises and let people know when you can't?
- Do you help people without thinking about?
- Does your behaviour fit your archetype?

What are you good at and what do you need to improve on? Think of other ways you need to improve your behaviour to build your brand, stand out and create happiness.

Part 2: See yourself in others and put yourself in the shoes of at least 5 people that you meet or see every day. Ask yourself, what are their hopes? What do they worry about? What could you have in common?

You may notice people smile at you, make sure you smile back. This is a great way to build connection and happiness. The more we connect, the easier it is to build our brands. Now think about your ideal client, family members, customer and / or employer. How can you put yourself in their shoes and build rapport?

Networking is another essential component when ensuring your brand shows up. It is also a great way to find and connect with opportunities. According to the Imperial College London's careers website, it is estimated that 75% of posts for jobs are generally filled though the hidden job market. This means you have to get out there and network. This activity is no longer only reserved for the entrepreneurs amongst us. A large number of jobs are secured via networking, so your network is your net worth as they say.

You can network both online and offline. We have discussed how to use your elevator pitch to make instructions both off and online, now it is time to start putting it into practice.

There are so many natural and easy ways to break the ice at face-to-face events and get a conversation started:

- Join the loner - Yep, that one standing alone in the corner, staring into his or her drink. Go up to ask if you can join them and introduce yourself and ask them how they are finding the event.

- Give a compliment - We all love compliments, especially when we are feeling insecure. So find something you like and let them know it.
- Just say hello - Sometimes, the easiest way to meet someone is to offer a handshake and simply introduce yourself with confidence.
- At the food table - Waiting in line for the food at an event is a great opportunity to start a conversation. Ask them what they are thinking of getting or ask them to recommend something.

Keep the conversation going - I know what you're thinking, 'Yes, yes, that's all well and good, but how can I keep the conversation going after the initial question?' It's easy! Ask them what they do, people generally like to talk about themselves, so listen intently and keep mental notes. Once they tell you what they do, hopefully they will ask you what you do, and this is where you drop your elevator pitch. If you have things in common, make sure you exchange contact details, website, socials and follow these up within 3 days so that you can keep the conversation going.

29 / ONLINE NETWORKING

If someone has accepted your request to connect on social media, you need to start a conversation. Send your new connection a short message after connecting to introduce yourself and tell them why you wanted to connect. Mention things you have noticed from their profile that you have in common and feel free to ask them about their goals and interests. This will help make a stronger personal connection. Offer your support or to introduce them to someone in your network if needs be. Do not ask for anything from them unless it benefits them in some way.

When someone reaches out to you and asks to connect, make sure you message them immediately after accepting their request with a message thanking them for connecting and how great it is to meet them. Over time you can invite them, or they will naturally choose, to be more involved in what you do.

TASK

Go and identify places you can go for business, career, or personal pursuits and activities. Book tickets and put the dates in your diary and start seeing networking as a way to expand your horizons and happiness. You never know who you may meet.

30 / BRANDING ELEMENTS

For those of you that are looking to start or already have your own business, you will need to think about the branding for your brand. Your branding is the visual representation of you. Nowadays, this is usually online so I thought I would pop this section in now as we enter the online part of your happiness journey. Your branding elements could include:

Logo – This is your brand signature/identity and is often the first and most recognisable element of your branding. It needs to be distinctive, unique and recognizable so that it stands out amongst the crowd.

Font - Using fonts to create a stylish brand takes knowledge of how to use typography in ways that will lift your brand to another level. Refer to the brand seasonal personality section and quiz to assist you with this.

Brand icons and devices - Add brand character but are not essential. They do, however, explain processes and information easier. They can be used to explain your services, categories, products etc. They can be used across social media, websites, blogs, and other literature and physical assets such as pop-up banners.

Illustrations - Add style, flair and character that literally tells your people what you are all about in a purposeful way. You cannot have an illustration for illustration's sake though; it has to be there for a reason. If you are thinking of this as a brand element, look back at your vision statement. Do this when you are planning your typefaces as well.

Patterns and texture - Can be added to both what you wear and your branding to create impact, diversity, and to consolidate your brand and its message. Patterns are a great way for your subordinate season to create something unique.

What patterns and prints align with you:

- Spring - Polka dots, ditsy florals, busy, energetic, random patterns, soft stripes with an element of movement that provides energy.
- Summer - Go for elegant, softly flowing watercolour stripes or the faded, floaty, airy, and graceful, delicate lines and soft structure.
- Autumn - Think of nature such as bark, wood, leaf and stone. Hand drawn or solid lines often featuring nature or the past.
- Winter - Dramatic, geometric, minimal strong bold lines and animal prints all create a strong impact.

DIY YOUR BRANDING ASSETS OR WORK WITH A CREATIVE

Your logo or photos are often the first and last thing clients see. They could be placed on your website, social media, promotional literature, or receipt at the end of a purchase. Your logo, if you decide to have one, should be dynamic, unique, confident, time-less, and strong. It should also be simple, distinctive, and well designed. Your logo, videos and photography are areas that you may want to bring in the professionals.

When I was working with a design team to discuss the visual look of my personal brand I already knew the brand colours and style of photography and video I wanted to use. I just need support to bring it all together with typography and a logo fami-ly. This made the process a lot easier for them and they were able to turn around my designs in two weeks rather than the usual 8 -12 weeks and I loved the first and only design that I was shown.

I had a call to discuss some key messages and personality I want to present and completed a questionnaire which included ques-tions about what I do, what I liked, what you didn't like and what I wanted for your brand etc. This enabled the designer to really get a strong idea of who I was and what I wanted to repre-sent. I completed a Pinterest board with lots of visual images for them to use as stimulation and inspiration. They used the answers to my questions and a Pinterest board as a brief and I noticed my designer popping up in unusual places, my social media lives, comments on posts etc. She was basically doing her research on what my visual strategy should be.

It was very reassuring knowing that I had a professional that had my back and that she was getting a better understanding of my personal brand. The process was really simple and that was because I knew who I was and what I wanted to put across so she was able to come up with a dynamic family of logos, sub logos and accompanying elements.

Working with third parties can be challenging. When working with my creative team it is always effective for my client because we really get to know a client so that we can deliver the best work. It's quite funny when I was working with one of my photographers at the brand shoot for the promo shoots for this book. I sat down on the sofa in my little gold dress holding what was a prototype book smiling sweetly into the camera and I heard the shutter click once. She took one picture then looked at her display.

I thought to myself this is not right. I was trying to be like all the other authors who I had seen images of and it just didn't feel right. I then did one of my funky more dynamic poses and she hit the shutter. It cracked about 10 times for one pose. She looked up at me and said "That's better, I was wondering, where are we going with this"

She knew I wasn't showing up as myself. I was trying to be somebody else but when I let my natural instinct kick in and let myself go I was able to shine. So I want you to remember we shine from within and you do not need to be showing up as anyone else, your branding needs to show your unique self. So just do you boo!

TASK – REVIEW YOUR VISUAL BRANDING

If you currently have a logo, photography or videos, it's time to evaluate them to ensure that they are consistent across all your on and offline platforms. Ask yourself the following questions and note the answers in your journal or notebook:

1. What are the typefaces, colours and devices communicating about you?
2. Does it have the impact you want?
3. Are you happy with the elements?
4. Do you need to refine any elements?
5. Is it fit for purpose?
6. Does it support your brand message?
7. Does it give you the confidence and professionalism you deserve?
8. Is it going to get you to where you want to be?
9. Do you need to tweak it?
10. Do you need to scrap it totally and emerge with something you will be proud of?

CREATING YOUR VISION & BRIEF

Pulling all your brand elements ideas together is fun and a great way to see how they work as a whole, as well as the full impact of your vision for happiness. Brand briefing boards are a great way to share your vision in visual representation with a professional. They also give you the opportunity to review all your ideas together and make sure your brand has depth and personality. With all your ideas and inspiration being in one place, you will be able to easily see how they work as a whole, and this will stop you changing things too often.

A brand board brief is useful to share with designers or your team as they develop. It will help a creative professional know more about you and ensure that your brand is represented consistently across all marketing messaging. As well as your brand elements, you may want to include your vision and values, the creative brief, colour palette and guidelines on what you want and any design work you may have mocked up

TASK - CREATING YOUR HAPPINESS VISION

Prepare, or develop further, a brand board about you. This could be on Pinterest, Canva, Pic Collage, in a scrapbook or cork board. Call it, 'This is me and my happiness" and should include the following at the least:

- Mission Statement.
- Target audience and what you do.
- Brand colours you like, linked to your brand values.
- Fonts you like.
- Logos you like.
- Words that inspire you and relate to your brand.
- Images you like

When I did this to brief my designer, this is the finished brand board she presented me with. There were about 90 or so images for reference and she used this, together with what she found out about me online, to create it. I totally fell in love with it at first sight. The colours, the image energy of the videography and photography.

I didn't notice that the word used to present my font was 'Happy'. At the time that I went through my branding process I didn't even know the title of my book but it's in total alignment don't you think?

MAIN LOGO DESIGN

COLOUR PALETTE

ALTERNATE STYLES & ICONS

FONTS

Selva

ABCDEFGHIJKLMNOPQRSTUVWXYZ
abcdefghijklmnopqrstuvwxyz

Montserrat

ABCDEFGHIJKLMNOPQRSTUVWXYZ
abcdefghijklmnopqrstuvwxyz

YVONNE PHILIP

31 / PHOTOGRAPHY AND VIDEO

Beautiful photography can unlock and transform your brand. You not only feel great when you see a standout picture of yourself, but it also makes others feel the same about you. Photo and video plays a huge part in your brand identity as it will show up on your website, blog, stationery, social media, and literature etc. It captures the essence of your brand in a snap shot or moving image.

Photography and video are the most powerful way to communicate your brand in my opinion. Why? Because your audience can really get an idea of who you are and what you offer. Remember 55% of a first impression is visual so if online, doing presentations and running adverts for your business with a dynamic still or moving image can often say more than words.

According to HubSpot 54% of consumers are looking for video content and 95% of marketing professionals say they got new business through video.

You do not need to be a business or freelancer to have a photo or videoshoot. Nowadays videos are often used for job applications and Boudoir type photoshoots can really build confidence so let's drive in.

Video and photography, although different, are very similar in terms and process. With my experience as a Model, Producer and Director of productions under my social enterprise and also the 1st Assistant Director on a feature film I thought I would take a little of your time to discuss this.

The process comes in three part:

1. Pre-Production

2. Production

3. Post production

Pre-Production - is your planning stage. Here you will need to think about the look and feel you want and how long it will take to capture the images or footage. You will also need to think about the footage you need, locations, outfits, props and a script / questions if the video has a voice over or interview. You may want to book a creative team of professionals to support you. The creative professionals you may need include a Creative Director, Photographer or Videographer/Editor depending if you are taking photos or recording video. You may also require a personal stylist, make-up artist and hairstylist.

The pre-production planning is the most important part of the process. Doing this effectively will ensure you have a happy, less stressful shoot.

TASK - PLANNING FOR YOUR SHOOT

To start the pre-production faze ask yourself the following questions:

1. Describe your brand, personality, values in 3 words?
2. What is unique and different about you?
3. Who do you work with and why?
4. What is your story and how can you use it with props and via the location you use.
5. What is the message you want to send and why is it so important?
6. What is the process you take your clients through, how do you work with them?
7. How do you want to be viewed and portrayed by your target audience?
8. What do you do with your spare time outside of work or business?
9. How and where are you planning to use the images or finished video?
10. What are your happiness, life, work and business goals for the next 6 - 12 months.

The answers to these questions will assist you in putting a brief together for your creative team or yourself to follow if you are self-shooting or shooting with a friend or family member. It's also a great way to start your shoot schedule which is a timetable for the day and also a list of shots that you need.

Production - is the shooting stage. When planning your outfits for the shoot production day most people stress and worry about what to wear. As a stylist I would say wear something that represents the new happier you are becoming and the personal brand you want to share with the world. The idea is for you to feel as comfortable as possible and feel like a star.

In terms of colour, you do not need to wear your brand colours but I would advise you to bring them into your outfits choices as they will ensure a consistent feel with the other brand elements. Even if you decide to wear natural tones a pop of colour is great but be careful that you do not clash with the background or location. A really simple way to do this is through your accessories. Items such as your jewellery, a scarf, coloured props or shoes will make all the difference.

Your outfits should include shoes, accessories and jewellery but what you wear will depend on your personality and brand. Your outfits should elevate your brand. I hear so many people say, "wear what you feel comfortable in" and yes that is true but I feel comfortable in jogging bottoms and a hoodie but that does not really represent my business and personal brand. Although I do show up this way on social media, for professional shoots this would be a no no for my brand. So, if you decide not to work with a personal stylist make sure you choose outfits that take you the extra mile. This will not only translate in the images and footage but also make you feel amazing.

I like to get bang for my buck at a shoot and I want to wear the most amount of looks in the least amount of time. With this in mind I always advise my client to wear an outfit that you can mix and match, i.e: a change of jacket, shoes, bag, top, jewellery can bring a whole different look and more images to play with. When packing make sure everything is ironed and use a suit carrier if you have one. Group outfits together so that you are not wasting time looking for items. Even take pictures of them so that you don't forget anything.

Make-up on the day and skin care leading up to the shoot day is always a good idea. You want your skin to look as flawless as possible. You don't have to change your look dramatically, you want to still look like you, just more evenly toned and refined.

If you wear make-up, think about a look that will align with you. If you don't wear makeup go for a natural look so that you still feel like you and people still recognise you. It's all about looking and feeling your best and confident when you look at yourself. Make sure you have moisturising cream on hand for the odd dry patch of skin that may pop up during the day and don't forget to polish your hand and toe nails if they are going to be on show.

Work through the shot list that you prepared during the pre-production stage. The shots or footage if video should tell the story of your brand and entice your audience to stop, look or listen. Relax and remember you earnt this just by being you. So give yourself the permission to be free and enjoy your moment in the spotlight.

SELF-SHOOTING V WORKING WITH A PROFESSIONAL.

I still self shoot, taking some photos on my mobile for social media but there is nothing like working with a professional. The quality of the finished product and your reduced stress level will work for you more than the cost. When you get them back and start using them for press, on your website or just to have the pictures in your home it will be worth it. They will take care of everything for you and this will lead to a more relaxed and enjoyable creative process.

If you are concerned about the cost, don't be. Often professionals have doubled up on their skills. For example I am the Stylist and also the Creative Director on my Seasonal Style Shoots. My other creatives also double up on skills for example hair and makeup, video camera and editing etc. So it does not have to break the bank especially as this option is also delivered as a group day if you decide to work with me. This has a number of benefits, you will be able to meet new people and network, have a fun day out where you won't even feel like you are working in addition to it being cost effective.

Post production - is the stage when everything is brought together. Your photos will be edited and retouched slightly. Heavy retouching can be expensive so try to get things near perfect on the shoot day. In terms of video this is when all your individual footage is pieced together to create one seamless piece. Adding music will take your video content to the next level and a text graphic as an intro and outro adds that professional touch.

You can access my suggested standard shot list for personal brand photoshoots in the resources section. This list is not limited and you may want more, less or different photos depending on your needs. You can download it by visiting www.yvonnephillip.com/book

REFLECTION

Do you think having a photo or video shoot will help your success and happiness? Use your journal to note down how you will use visual assets and where they will benefit you. Photos and video have seasonal personalities to, which will yours have:

- Spring - Fun images full of colour, light, and brightness whilst being warm and soft.
- Summer - Images have a softness to them and are cool, calm, and relaxed with a hazy lighting.
- Autumn - Photography has a motivating energy about it with a rich, intense, natural feel.
- Winter - Images will be clean, bright, crisp, intense, understated and edgy.

Remember, your logo, photography and videography are areas where you should consider bringing in the professionals if you want to be taken seriously and create true happiness via your visual branding.

32 / YOUR WEBSITE AND PRESENCE

Your web presence is a random series of online sites, mentions and posts that can be out of date and present you in the wrong light. So, the first thing we are going to do is conduct a web audit.

TASK

On someone else's computer, with no settings specific to you, open Google and type in your full name in inverted commas i.e. 'June Jones'. What do you find? More importantly, is this what you want people to see about you?

If you do not like what you see and read, you can:

1. Take legal action, which can be time consuming and expensive.
2. Get more active online to get positive activity that pushes the negativity lower down the page rankings. A great way to do this is via a blog in your own name with

regular posts so that, after a while, you will be at the top of page one if you don't have a common name.

3. Hire an online reputation manager who will do the above for you.

Potential clients may expect you to have a website but with the power of social media, a website is not always needed. It does, however, give you a professional presence for people to check you out, your hobbies, interests, and opinions. If you are in business, they would want more information about you and what you do, products you sell or have created.

If you are looking for work, you can use a website as a blog to prove your knowledge of the industry by proving you are keeping up to date with your sector. It can make you more visible to employers but should not have too much self-promotion that will send the wrong message to a potential boss. A personal site is a great compliment to your CV and allows you to bring all your online activity together in one place, with links to your social media in addition to blogs, photographs, audio, and video clips etc.

A personal and professional business site can also direct people to other people's content that relates to you. You can also be featured on the website of trade associations, industry bodies or charities your brand relates to or supports.

If you are not a professional web designer, you may need help. You can, however, build your own site. This is an easy way to get started however some self-build sites have limitations and may require plugin apps to optimise your site for search engines. If you are not tech savvy, a web developer can build on this for you and as they will not be building a site from scratch, it will save you some money. It should only cost you a couple of hundred pounds.

If you want your site to be a full marketing machine, you may want to opt for a platform such as: Kartra or Clickfunnels or a bespoke website created by a developer. These sites provide all you need if you want a fully functioning online business. This means you will not have to use lots of different software options for the different requirements of running a fully functional online business.

Either way, your website can communicate your talents, skills and experience through text, images and illustration, video and more. Having a website is like a window into you and what you have to offer as a business and employee.

Make sure your images and fonts evoke the season and values your brand presents. It is also important to make sure the style and tone of voice reflects the way you speak and the archetype and personality you want to evoke. Make your site useful so that visitors add it to their favourites. Here are the 10 things your website should include:

1. About me - Your about me page helps people to connect with you personally and professionally. It should include your biography with a clear professional profile picture of you looking into the camera.
2. Services / products sales page - This page(s) should include all information to the products and services. This is the sales page(s) with info on your products, services and should promote the benefits as well as the features of your offer, along with links to buy or get in contact.

3. Lead magnet - A downloadable item of free content is always a great way to provide tips and guidelines on how to solve the problem that your audience has. What you give is up to you as long as it is of value and it is backed up with an email sign up and optional sequence so you can start to grow your marketing list, follow up and relationship build. Ensure it is data protection compliant for the territories you operate in.

4. Frequently Asked Questions (FAQs) - This reduces the number of questions that you get asked all the time and minimises the number of people that contact you about the same thing, so it is great for time management.

5. Contact details - This could be a contact form, email address, telephone number or physical address.

6. Social media links - Assist customers with their buying decisions by adding links to your social media accounts. Make sure your accounts are consistent with your website in terms of its visual branding to ensure cohesions across the brand.

7. Links - Give people reason to revisit your website and enhance their connection with you. The quality and values of the site(s) should be the same or better than yours.

8. Portfolio and / or testimonies - Add value to your brand reputation and credibility by including testimonies, case studies, and quotes from previous clients or people you have worked with.

9. An obvious call to action. Let your online visitors know what you want them to do with a clear request for them to take action. What do you want them to do? Call now for a free quote, sign up, book a call, follow me etc.

Make sure this stands out by using special buttons or highlighting the text.

10. Terms of business / privacy policy - Include your business terms and also privacy policy in relation to the territories you operate in.

A few other things to consider;

- Blog/Vlog or Podcast - New fresh, quality content is a great way to keep your site continually updated and a reason to come back.

- A simple, sensible web address - Your domain name is an extension of your brand so don't make it complicated. Try to secure a .com domain, or for non-profits or organisations, a .org domain where possible.

- An easily navigated site map - A site map is great for guiding visitors to the information they want. Make it easy for them with clear links to the most important pages.

- Search Engine Optimization (SEO) - Use keywords in your text and plenty of links, to make sure your website is found by search engines and also name your page titles and URLs correctly.

- A secure hosting platform - Use a trustworthy hosting company to keep the hackers out and your content up and running. Having a secure hosting platform is essential.

Ensure your email sign off and signature is in line with your branding. It should include your name, job title, and strapline. It can also include your logo and any awards, associations, or qualifications you have. Don't forget to make it easy for people to find you and investigate further by adding your web address, contact details and social media links or handles.

Once you have completed your site, get someone to check the grammar and spelling. Show it to a few people before it goes live and ask them:

1. What is their first impression?
2. How does it make them feel?
3. How easy is it to navigate?
4. How does it look on a mobile phone?

But most importantly, how does it make you feel?

REFLECTION

Is your website consistent in terms of colours, fonts, and tone of voice, as the rest of your online and offline presence?

TASK

1. Set up a Google Alert for your name so that when new content about you is published, you know about it.
2. Give your website an audit. What needs to be improved?
3. If you do not have a website, make sure you include the above when you start to build one.

33 / SOCIAL MEDIA

As we move into social media, this section will be great for those who want to share their 'Go Happy Yourself' journey for personal use. It will also benefit those that want to use social media for business and marketing. Either way, you are a business of one remember, so you need to let people know that you are out there, your knowledge and what you are up to within reason.

To be effective at online marketing, it is best for you to know what you want to achieve and the archetype you want to evoke. Social media allows you to get your message out to a mass audience. If you want your social media content to have a real impact, you need to make sure the campaign goals align with the ambitions of you and your company, if you have one. For instance, do you want to:

- Improve brand awareness: Increase your follower count, your mentions, retweets, shares etc
- Generate new leads: Increase the download of content, to create new leads through social media and clicks on your lead-generation posts.

- Drive traffic to your website: Check referral traffic coming from social media in your Google analytics dashboard, along with things like clicks on social posts and bounce rate for social traffic.

To be effective, your social media should provide either inspiration, education, or humour in your posts. Your online presence should also have consistency, build engagement, and create conversion. Each post / piece of content should include a call to action, this could include: download my freebie, join my group, send me a message, or comment below for example.

SOCIAL MEDIA GUIDES

You'll want to establish a guide to keep your content consistent. Although there's no one-size-fits-all guide to content, ideally your social posts should be designed to create emotional bonds with your audience. That means establishing a unique personality and tone of voice.

1. Find your voice: Think about what you want your personality to be like and try to make sure it aligns with the platform you've chosen. For instance, a professional tone is more appealing on LinkedIn, while a playful tone might work on Snapchat or TikTok.
2. Tell a story: Social media is about engaging with your audience, so make sure that you have a strategy for sharing content that aligns with your values. For instance, you should only share content that's relevant to your industry, aligns with your ethics and highlights your brand purpose and personality.

3. Know your competition: Being effective in your social media content strategy is all about making sure you're better than the competition, whether you're in official business or looking for work. Figure out what some of the main people are doing, then decide how you can do it better.

So, you have a good idea of who you're speaking to and may have an idea of where your social strategy is taking you. Now you need to know what kind of content you'll create. Your aim should be to design content that's relevant to your business and its values. Don't post content for the sake of it.

Since you know your audience and where they spend their time, why not find out more about what they want to see from your brand. Questionnaires, challenges, video series, newsletters, and polls are fun and effective ways to start engaging your audience.

Keywords help you to target your content. You can monitor hashtags or branded keywords to easily feed content viewed by your ideal client. Here you can see exactly what people are saying about a specific keyword or how they're using a certain hashtag. This will help you build your content strategy more effectively by knowing exactly what to target.

Then you can see how well people engage with your keyword afterward. Looking at what comes up when you type your focus market into different social media platforms will not only help you to figure out your competitors, but also provide you with alternative keywords and hashtags.

Adverts can be used across all platforms except Snapchat if you set up a company / business page. Although this may change, it is advised to first build your reputation and confidence organically before moving to adverts. Adverts are quite simple to create but contracting an Ads Managers with a good track record may save you money in the long run. Some can however be expensive and provide little return on your investment. Do your research to ensure ads are the right investment for you.

Hashtags can be used to assist your audience in finding you. They group posts together so they are searchable. Use hashtags that your audience will be looking for, not what your competitor will use. For example, would your client be looking for a #MarketingCoach or #MarketingTips

Optimise your profile so it is fully completed to include a picture, cover image, and bio where allowed. Use your brand elements! On some social media platforms such as LinkedIn, you can also put in PDF documents, videos, and photos to your profile. With regard to Instagram, you may want to invest in a LinkTree account if you do not have a website. With this app, you can have one link which links to a series of your other content, downloads, and sites.

CREATING AND STRUCTURING YOUR CONTENT

Social media is full of communities for you to tap in to, to enhance your 'Go Happy Yourself' journey. Your content can consist of, images, videos, quotes, testimonies, short & long form copy, and articles across the various different neighbourhoods. These neighbourhoods include your main feed, stories, reels, and going live etc.

There are various ways to structure a piece of content. You can use your brand story or the hero's journey as mentioned before, I particularly like to use the AIDA method. This is a basic, but very effective, marketing advertising concept to assist you in structuring your copy.

A - Attention

The first part of your copy needs to grab the audience's attention.

I - Information

Provide them with the information about your product or service.

D - Desire

Create desire for them to buy or take action by stating the features, not the benefits.

A - Action

Inspire them into the relevant action you would like them to take.

TASK – DRAFTING CONTENT WITH IMPACT

Step 1 - Let's take some time to break this down with a short exercise to get the creative juices flowing:

- List 5 pains and needs of your ideal client / company / employer etc.
- List 5 aspirations and desires they have.
- List 5 transformation / solutions you provide for them to overcome or achieve the above.
- List 5 common values you think you share.

- List hobbies and interests that could create connections.
- What types of action(s) do you want your audience to take after your posts?

Step 2 – Now, take one topic out of the 5 and think about a post you could produce for it:

- What form will the post take: video, photo, text etc
- What is the objective of the post; Inspire, Educate, Amuse (humorous)?
- What will your call to action be?

Step 3 - draft a piece of content in your journal that introduces the happiness you are creating for yourself and others. If you need structure, use the AIDA method or story brand structure from earlier.

34 / CONSIDERING CONSISTENCY

The key to your brand's elevation and happiness is consistency. This consistency should be across all areas of your life, business or career but in this section are going to continue to focus on social media. Being active consistently can be overwhelming and totally tiring so I will be discussing how you can reduce that now and also in the self-management pillar of this book a little later on.

- Confused people do not engage, buy, invest or employ, so make sure the content you put out is in line with the archetype you want to portray. If not you will send mixed messages and confuse your audience.
- Make sure your content is put out consistently each week. Do not commit to posting when you are not sure you will be able to maintain it. Push yourself, but if putting out content 3 times a week is all you can do, make sure it is high quality and you show up when you say you will.

- Networking and visibility are an important part of this too. It helps to engage and grow your audience and create business and job opportunities.

You also need to consider how you are going to manage yourself and stay consistent. A social media strategy and plan can help with this and should be part of your overall marketing strategy. Here's a quick summary of the process:

- Decide what audience your content is targeting.
- Choose a topic and a platform for your content.
- Decide which kind of content you're going to share (image, infographic, video, blog post, update, etc.)
- Research the best time to post on your platform of choice.
- Evaluate when your target audience is online.

Once you've researched and decided all of this, it may be best to take the time each week to schedule your posts in advance. This will ensure you never miss a chance to engage with your audience. You can use a scheduling app for this however some platforms allow you to schedule on the platform.

Share your stories, client pains, your desires, and the transformation you create or are creating for yourself and them. You may even want to theme each day of the week. Thinking of content to create can sometimes be tricky so let us do a quick task to generate a few ideas:

TASK:

Part 1 - Visit: Awareness Days https://www.awarenessdays.com

and or United Nations website:

https://www.un.org/en/sections/observances/united-nations-observances/index.html

Part 2 - Go through the site and select awareness and observances days, months and weeks that will resonate with your 'Go Happy Yourself' activities and audience. Think of their pains, desires, values, and hobbies etc. Detail them in your journal.

Part 3 - Draft some copy based on the awareness and observances from your viewpoint. Think about the words, images, videos and illustrations you will use to put your brand message across.

35 / ENGAGEMENT AND CREATING COMMUNITY

You can strengthen your brand and the bonds with your social media connections and turn them into loyal friends and fans that may refer people to you. Research says it takes between 7 - 21 touches and points of contact for someone to consider buying from or investing in you, so you need to engage in conversations to build relationships.

In addition to asking questions, doing polls and challenges etc, you can also respond to queries in instant messages, reshare or engage with content, and share customer feedback.

TRACKING PERFORMANCE & MAKING ADJUSTMENTS

When you publish your content, you will need to track your strategy and make changes. The most common areas you should be interested in tracking are engagement, reach and conversions. Here are some of the things you'll need to look out for:

1. Engagement: How many people are connecting with you online? Think about retweets, shares, mentions

and clicks on social media posts. Comments and shares can be very important too and also help to get your posts pushed by the social media platform.

2. Reach: How many people are engaging with your content? Measure this by looking at how many new connections or followers you've gathered over the last month or so.

3. Conversions: Is your social media content strategy prompting sales? You will need to use analytics to help you measure how many valuable leads are connecting with your company thanks to your posts.

TASK

It is important that you have a Social Media Content Strategy to help you plan and deliver your message to the world. Draft a simple social media content strategy for the next 1 - 6 months. You do not have to plan a detailed calendar of exactly what you are going to post on each day and on which platform or at what times etc, but it may be an idea for you to plot key dates in a month-to-view calendar so you can clearly see activity. This will not only help you to plan this overview clearly, but also focus you when you start to get more specific.

1. What is the aim of your social media strategy?
2. What are your key social media platforms going to be?
3. How often will you post?
4. What will your posts be about?

5. Can you develop a wider campaign around this and when will these take place?

6. What will your call to action be and where will you lead them next?

7. You may want to start a Social Media Planner (but this is not essential at this stage).

8. Will you be using a scheduling app? If so, what will you be using?

9. Bring all your brand elements together and provide three examples of the type of posts you will produce moving forward: the posts can be quotes, images, testimonies... and you must include the copy that will be placed with it?

10. How will you evaluate the success of the strategy and when?

Remember, consistency is key, so let's get social!

36 / BLOGGING, VLOGGING AND PODCAST

Now it is time to make your brand stand out and get visible in addition to presenting. At this stage, a great way to do this is via blogging, vlogging or podcasting. This is also known as long form content. They create direct and genuine connections with your potential employers, friends, clients and customers and can be highly converting over time. If linked to your website, having regular, long form content can also keep people coming back to your site, thus boosting it in search engine searches.

The first thing you need to do is decide if you want to blog, vlog or podcast. So, answer the following about yourself. What do you prefer to do?

- Do you like to write?
- Do you like to speak and be seen?
- Do you like to speak but don't want to be seen on camera?

If you like to write, starting a blog may be best for you. If you like to speak and don't mind being seen, a vlog may be best for you.

However, if you do not want to be seen on camera, a podcast would be best. The process of each is very similar but let's go through each one in turn.

BLOGGING

A blog is a type of website or extension of your site that mainly focuses on written content called blog posts. Your blog can be written from a personal or professional perspective, and it allows your audience and target audience to connect directly and allow readers to respond via a comments section. Interacting with your readers in the comments section helps to further the connection.

This connection allows you to interact and share ideas with other like-minded people. It also allows you to build trust with your readers. Having the trust and loyalty of your readers also opens up the door to making money from your blog and creating sales. With a blog you can:

- Make money from home. Blogging can be a form of passive or semi passive income as you can link and recommend products and receive an affiliate commission.
- Share your story. A blog allows you to have a voice, be heard and get noticed. You can share your story with the world if you so choose. You can use it as a diary to write about your daily experiences so that friends, family, and others can all be a part of your life.
- Recognition for yourself or your business. No, you probably won't have people asking for your autograph or photographers following you around, but a successful blog can gain you a lots of recognition in

your respective field. Many bloggers are known as experts just because of their blogs, and some have even got PR, book and movie deals based on them.

- Find a community. Blogging is interactive, so it is a great way to connect with people who share the same interests as you are. You can teach people based on your experience, and also learn from them as well.

You can name your blog differently from your website if you are keeping it separate, but make sure it is descriptive, catchy, memorable and will rank in keywords. Also, add a really brief description in the title tag. This is so that potential readers can instantly tell what your blog is about just from the name.

So, what can your blog content be about? Here are a few ideas:

- Q&A video
- Transformation video
- Tips or tricks for (insert topic)
- How to
- Information
- Event coverage
- Share a skill talent
- Behind the scenes
- Facts about you
- A personal struggle overcome
- Travel Stories
- What's in your bag
- Make..
- What charity is important to you
- Interviews
- Day in the life

- Top secrets (on a given topic)
- Top mistakes
- Future channel plans
- Lifestyle stories

TASK

Take some time to think about 12 ideas that you can produce long form content about. Once you have finished you will have 1 years' worth of content ideas if you plan to post monthly, or 3 months' worth of posts if you decide to post weekly. Some of the things you have already found out about yourself on your 'Go Happy Yourself' journey so far could help you.

VLOGGING

The reason why you should vlog and blog are the same. Vlogging is great for you if you do not mind being on camera and are looking to save time and resources by having the flexibility to post your content in multiple formats. For example:

1. You can create a video and share it to a video hosting site.
2. You can then get your video transcribed to text and / or audio for an email or blog post.
3. You can then post it to your blog and /or podcast

Alternatively, you can:

1. Take a screen capture picture
2. Edit the video / audio into a shorter clip.
3. Post this to your social media as part of your content strategy.

To get started, you will need a camera that has the ability to record a video, such as a smartphone, tablet, webcam or DSLR with a good quality microphone. You will also need editing software, laptop/computer, tripod and may need a lighting set-up. If you are going to go down this line of standing out and raising your visibility, it may be good for you to make the investment. If you do not have the money to invest yet, don't let this stop you from taking action!

WRITING AND STRUCTURING YOUR WRITTEN AND VIDEO CONTENT

Hook - The hook is a small snippet of video that entices the viewer to watch the full video. It does not give away your solutions but gives them a reason to continue watching to the end.

Intro – The intro is where you frame the problem and let the viewer know what you are going to be talking about and who it will help them.

Main content - Once you've introduced your video, in the main body of the content you need to let your audience know how this problem is affecting you and your viewers. Then offer solutions with examples on how you found this solution. Is it easy to implement? Take around four to five minutes to address your solution and give examples of how it works in practice.

Outro - Your outro shouldn't just be about signing off in your unique way with some lovely music and visuals if possible. This is the point at which you can ask your audience a question with a 'call to action'. What do you want them to do next? You don't just want to be giving them free advice; there has to be a return or reward for you too. It is also great to sign off in a signature way. For example, I sign off by saying 'Stay true to you and ciao for now' this makes you memorable and can also deepen your message.

TASK

Use the points above to outline a piece of content on a subject you have chosen earlier.

FILM A VLOG

Alright, so now you have a camera to record a vlog and upload it. Now it's time to actually start vlogging. You already know the topics that you can talk about in terms of transformations, but you can also film what you do every day, your hobbies, what's on your mind, do challenges, or anything else.

Here are some tips for recording your first vlog. It will also come in handy for video and photoshoots:

1. Don't overthink it and relax: Have a skeleton or notes but don't over plan it. Just start recording and say naturally what's within the brief that you have created. Being spontaneous and reacting to your natural

environment is great when vlogging and for your happiness.

2. Good lighting and audio quality: If you do not have a vlogging camera with a light, make sure you put the phone or camera in front of a window or sunlight facing into the location and present so you are looking towards the window / sun. You can also get a ring light for your face. Make sure to speak clearly and don't leave any long silences if you don't plan to edit unless they are for dramatic effect.

3. Interact with your audience: vlogging is a great way to connect on a more personal level. Make sure to respond to comments and ask their opinion to things that you talk about.

4. Sign off with a unique personal phrase: This helps you personalise your videos. Most successful vloggers have their own unique phrase they use to end the vlog and often at the start to.

EDIT AND UPLOAD YOUR VLOG

Editing makes your vlog look more professional but is not essential. As you grow you can learn this skill or work with a videographer and / or editor. If you want to do it yourself, there are a lot of free (and paid) apps that can do this, but do not let the lack of tech stop you. Just record your content straight to camera and upload it anyway. If you have an Apple computer, you can use iMovie and if you have a Windows computer, you can use Windows Live Movie Maker. Luckily, there are plenty of tutorials online to learn how to use this software. Sites like Vimeo and YouTube are great for hosting your vlogs and you can also link these back to your website.

PODCASTING

Podcasts are more convenient than blogs and vlogs for your clients and audience. They can listen to them at the gym, in the car and my personal favourite, whilst doing the housework. Podcasting is relatively new and is less saturated than blogs or vlogs.

The concept of your Podcast should be connected to your brand. You will need to think about the name and format but before that, let's think about one of the fundamentals and that is your 'why'. Why are you starting a podcast (blog/vlog) and what is your podcast about?

So, what is your goal or the purpose of your content? Is it to:

1. Generate leads?
2. Be recognised as an authority and leader in an industry?
3. Share a message?
4. Have fun?

Once you have this, do a little market research of what others are doing, to work out ways you feel you can be different, improve and be unique.

Podcasts come in different formats, from single host to scripted stories to in depth interviews and news recaps. Choose a format and content length that suits you:

- Blog: 500 words average
- Vlog: 10 - 20 Minutes
- Podcast: 20 - 30 minutes

Podcasts are quite cost effective to start with. Like vlogging, you can start with just your phone and headphones (with micro-phone) and grow from there. Once you have recorded your content, you will need to make some edits and adjust the sound quality. You can use Audacity (free) and Garageband (free) to do this.

Whatever platform you decide to put your long form content out on, you need to do your research and watch, read, and listen to others. However I don't want you to start comparing yourself to others. Once you have your topic, write an outline of bullet points that you can follow. This will stop you from rambling and ensure you and any co-host are on the same page.

Record in quite small spaces, rather than larger ones. If it is not soundproof make sure it has lots of material to absorb or diffuse the sound and echoes. However, if there is a little interference, it can always be cleaned up post-production. If you are using a professional microphone, try to use a pop shield and set it up to the side and angled towards your mouth. This will avoid any air pop, lip smacking and give you a more natural tone. So, now you are ready, grab a drink and start recording. Don't worry about stammers, mistakes, or a little silence, as they can be edited out.

Let your content goals and your brand personality be your guide as you enter the editing phase. Will it be fast paced, short, conversational, interview or a monologue? Think about this before you start to cross fade and cut up your content so that it flows naturally after the edit.

REFLECTION

What do you think your show will be like for the seasons: Spring, Summer, Autumn, Winter. What would your content look, read and sound like for your archetype?

5 TIPS FOR ONLINE VISIBILITY

1.   Keep Going!

Your long form content will not have thousands of views at first but don't let that hold you back or stop you. Set a schedule for how often you want to upload and stick with that schedule no matter what. Keep networking with other YouTubers, bloggers, podcasters, and people on social media to see if you can collaborate with others and grow faster.

2.   Don't let negativity break your spirit

As you grow in views, listeners and mentions, you will also get some negative comments. Don't fear being judged. It's easy to criticise others but you're the one who is brave enough to write, film, record and upload yourself when others are too scared to so sit behind their keyboard spitting negativity. Don't let the negative comments get to you. You could just wonder how sad their life must be but it would be better for your happiness if you just focus on the positive comments and the achievements you have made.

3.   Use Royalty Free Music

Some sites will automatically check for any copyrighted songs and will mute the audio or take action if you use any copyrighted material. This can mean you are unable to monetize the video and after three strikes, they can also ban your account. To prevent any of this from happening you should always use royalty free music.

4. Test, Test, Test

Keep on testing and trying new things. Use feedback in the comments and your analytics to evaluate and analyse the success you are making along the way. Keep learning and improving as you launch each piece of content and create a happy little world for yourself and others.

5.   Promote your Blog, Vlog or Podcast

And my final tip is don't be shy about telling people about your long form content. By now, you have a brilliant brand, and it is worthy of showing off. You can promote your content effectively and for free by using; email marketing, social networks, Pinterest, your blog, your directories, your podcast, commenting on other blogs, linking to other content, guest posting, online forums and by posting frequently. Use a scheduling app to make your life easier.

TASK

Complete the outline and treatment for a long form piece of content.

PILLAR 3 - SELF-CARE AND MANAGEMENT

GROW AND SUSTAIN FOR CREDIBILITY

37 / WHY SELF-CARE AND SELF-MANAGEMENT MATTERS

So, we now have you looking fly and fabulous, and you are getting out there on and offline. What about how we act to get happy? From here, you can take your happiness and personal brand to another level and share your expertise and message to the larger numbers or people through:

- Sponsorship and partnerships.
- Starting to pursue media opportunities in the press.
- Taking part in TV appearances.
- Speaking and presenting on stages and at larger events, in person and online.
- Writing and publishing a book.

Now, I can hear you all screaming, 'I can't do that' and what I will say to you is, "you think you can't yet." You may not be ready and that is ok. I also cover these topics on my signature programmes, retreats and my 1:1 offerings. However, I have chosen instead to focus on the self-care element of the 'Go Happy Yourself' journey and how you are going to sustain and grow your brand and happiness. To do this, you need to be careful and consider your self-management techniques and life-style choices.

You see, as you get to greater levels of happiness and success, those feelings of being an imposter and self-limiting beliefs will return. They call it the 'up level devil' and there is a great intro book about this by Gay Hendricks called The Big Leap . At each stage of your development you will feel and have to face fear and you will have to get over or tame it to progress.

In addition to this, you may feel overwhelmed or burn yourself out as you climb the ladder of success to greater happiness. I did this when I was running my social enterprise. I was spending so much time focusing on everything and everyone else; my son, mother, partner, clients, funders and other stakeholders, that I was not giving to myself. I ended up giving from an empty cup and burning out. For my health, I had to make the decision to walk away from it. With this in mind, you must put in place the routines and rituals that nourish your mind, body, and soul. For example:

- Mind - meditation, journaling, reading, education and learning.
- Body - exercise, yoga, pilates, weightlifting, walking etc.
- Soul - social activities, hobbies, friends, family.

The third thing that is going to hinder your sustainable success is not learning how to handle other people that may stress you out and get in the way of your happiness, and how to control that. You know, that demanding or micro-managing boss or co-workers, maybe a family member or even a client.

Jane Edis is the creator of the playalong20 method and my
client. She helps recorder players who need accountability and
community to play ensembles. I sat down with Jane to discuss
the self-care and management of her journey.

Yvonne

Jane, could you tell everybody what you do?

Jane

When lockdown first occurred, I was working part time at IBM as an IT architect, which is my day job. That seamlessly moved into working online and I still do that today. Apart from that, I am also running an apartment in Lanzarote, which, of course, was completely shut down for 3 months. I also ran recorder ensemble lessons, which, of course, also had to be cancelled due to lockdown. So, at that point of my life, I just didn't know where to go! I pushed forward with moving my recorder group online, which meant I had to record all the music in advance for them to play along to. Then, as the summer wore on, I thought that other people might need this! So, I opened it up and did a taster session, which I posted on recorder groups on Facebook - and I now have 5 different sessions happening throughout the week with people all over the world! People joined the taster session from all over the place - Uzbekistan, Hong Kong, Australia, Canada - and it was very exciting. A good proportion of those people choose to come along to the sessions 1-2 times a week.

Yvonne

What I love about your business is that it is so niche. It is a genius idea to take this an international online business! I have supported you as an accountability pod leader. How did you find that pod?

Jane

The accountability pod was a weekly event during the 12-week course. The course itself is really quite intense and having that accountability every week and the chance to just catch up with people who were going through the same journey as you, made it more realistic to tackle it. With my particular niche, I felt very small compared to other people who already had large businesses and were talking about large sums of money. It was hard to see my way through without having that personal touch. It helped enormously as it kept the momentum going - otherwise it would have been so easy to drift off and think it wasn't for me. My imposter syndrome would have kicked in and I wouldn't have allowed myself to get to grips with the difficult bits that you need to push through in order to get it working. I am the type of person who needs accountability, needs community and I need people to talk to as I am working through things. I am a team worker really, but when you are doing a business that is just you, you have to build up your team around you. That is something that I have only recently realised - building up your team around you is what you need - and Yvonne is the voice in my head that is keeping me accountable. I find you refreshingly direct. If something needs saying, you say it, but in a very kind way. You are not putting people off or making them feel scared, which is perfect for me! I need someone to give me a little bit of a kick... but with positive encouragement.

Yvonne

We can all do it and, as you said, you were fearful being in a big crowd and sometimes your imposter syndrome kicks in, therefore you need the accountability. Is that the reason you decided to join The Success Sisterhood?

Jane

Over the last 18 months, I have done quite a bit of personal development and I came to recognise some of my traits, such as procrastination. The imposter syndrome only really became apparent to me when I started my music classes, as that was new to me as a business. Having realised that I do need that accountability and support when it comes to my procrastination struggles and overwhelm. I am trying to do an awful lot of business during my week's work - I have a lot of things going on - so it is a bit of a management nightmare. Understanding where the priorities need to be can be difficult, and that is when you want to talk to somebody rather than getting lost in a super long to do lists!

Why I joined The Success Sisterhood - you attract people who are the type of people who support each other through thick and thin - and that's exactly what I wanted to feel part of.

Yvonne

One of the reasons I set up The Success Sisterhood is that I know that solo female entrepreneurship can be very lonely. If you don't have community or work in collaboration with compassion (the 3 pillars of The Success Sisterhood), it can be very challenging. That is when you start suffering from overwhelm and self-limiting beliefs.

Jane

Immediately I saw the need for me because I know that in order for me to achieve my goals in a way that I can also maintain myself, I need community around me. In the past, I have tried to be Superwoman and I had a heart attack around 10 years ago.

Yvonne

Oh Jane, I never knew that. That is why I don't want women to get to that point. When I went through my burnout, I was nearly at that point. If I hadn't closed my business down, that probably would have happened to me. I was out for about a year.

Jane

Yeah, it was a massive wakeup call. I was working all week, had appointments, lots of activities happening and last-minute changes - but someone else took all that and did it instead - and guess what? They managed! They survived without me but in your mind, you think that you are necessary for everything and try to do everything. For me, it didn't work in the end and my body gave up.

Yvonne

The way I see it, is that we are all Superwomen, but we can only be that if we have self-management and manage our self-care. There has to be a blend and balance in our strategy, our style, and our self-care. There has to be all of them to make it work. There is never going to always be balance, but it's about recognising that out of balance feeling and knowing what to do to get it back where it needs to be.

Jane

I was tackling everything with a very particular sort of energy, and I don't think I was tapping into things that came from the heart. There are feminine energies that I hadn't even realised existed until I started doing personal development. Although I was never alone in any of my organisations, I did feel as though I needed to do it all myself for some reason. I did too much. It has been a journey since then. It was a wakeup call. I stopped doing anything for 3 months and then after that, I picked and chose what I wanted to do from there on. It stopped me for years, but I am now at the stage of personal development that allows me to get the balance right so that I can stay alive!

Yvonne

Absolutely! Literally. Thank you for sharing that with us as it is so powerful in terms of the message I want to send through my program. Your story was more detrimental to your health than mine and mine felt bad enough. Burnout can happen just like that, and it could happen to any of us. We don't know when it is going to hit us. That is what my program is all about. I want people to be able to achieve their dreams and their passions but also do it while they are enjoying themselves. We need to enjoy the success! A lot of us don't enjoy success as we are thinking about making money and moving on to the next thing. Have a reward in your goal setting plans!

Jane

Yes. I love the idea of the rewards in there as I don't think I was ever rewarding myself for anything! I spent my whole life beating myself up for not being able to do more!

Yvonne

Jane your story is amazing. You are investing in yourself now. Your business is going to grow, and I am going to be by your side, gently leading you forward and keeping you accountable. Of course, have some fun along the way!

Jane

Yes. To me, that is the best bit about having community. Some things can be terribly boring, but you have to just push through and it's nice to know you are not alone and other people are having to do the same thing. It makes such a big difference as you can easily think that you are the only one and it's just not true!

Yvonne

Absolutely. What you don't realise is that lots of other people are going through exactly the same thing, but because you are so tunnel visioned on what you are doing, you don't realise. That is why I built this community, so we can grow and succeed together, but also collaborate and have fun!

If you need support with your rituals and routines, download the Lifestyle Challenge and 10 steps to a healthier happier you for tips on a simple routine that you can implement. You can find it at visit www.yvonnephillip.com/book

39 / MOTIVATION

What have you identified that is going to hold you back? This is a question that you are going to have to continually ask yourself. The answers will lead you to your next level of happiness. You may be thinking of giving up and in need of a little motivation, but what you need is self-actualisation and accepting that you and your needs matter too. Once you have this, you can operate better in your life, career, and business. You will be more motivated, more productive, make better decisions and problem solve with better efficiency.

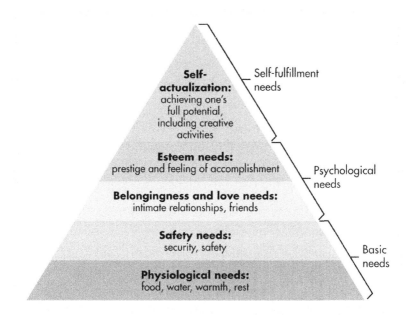

Maslow chart of hierarchy motivational needs © Simply Psychology

When you lack the energy or the mindset to get up and do something, what do you do? Your actions are based on a number of things. So let's look back to you having delivered at your best, you will have felt a sense of comfort and security. Maslow's hierarchy of needs highlights that if our basic needs are not being met, we will not be motivated to reach our full potential and happiness. With this in mind, you should always seek to make sure your needs are being met before anyone else. Yes, I mean your child(ren) too (within reason, of course), as long as they are safe, clean, fed, and happy, you need to think about you too, and keeping up with health habits and routines will help this. You see you cannot give from an empty cup, so you need to feed yourself first.

Have you noticed that some days you are on a roll, having all the get up and go and ticking off everything on your to do list. Other days you're flitting from task to task, not getting it together. When this happens, we need to think about what we are doing that is demotivating you. What is making you procrastinate and what will give you the well needed nudge, or 'kind kick' as my clients like to call it, to get the job done. There are 4 types of motivation:

- Extrinsic Motivation - Extrinsic motivation is motivation that comes from outside us. We basically have to do it, for example, because you are told to do something by your boss. You are paid a salary with benefits, and then have to do something when asked or told to do so.

- Intrinsic Motivation - Intrinsic motivation is done for internal reasons, for example, to align with values or simply for pleasure and because you like to do it. This is a sweet spot and finding a job or business that intrinsically motivates you is the key to happiness.

- Introjected Motivation - Introjected motivation is like intrinsic motivation. The main difference is that you may feel tension, guilt, or shame if the thing you need to do is not done.

- Identified Motivation - Identified motivation is where you know that something needs to be done but have not yet decided to do anything about it. With this type of motivation, you can get yourself or someone else to do something. This is called delegation which shall be covered later on in this section.

TASK

Which of the following are you going to add to the things you have already committed to, in order to keep you motivated. Go through the things you need to do and the actions you will take to create happiness. Identify what is going to motivate you to keep going from the following:

1. Convince yourself you want to do it - Reframing is one of the easiest things you can do to motivate yourself.
2. Take control - Remind yourself that you are in control of your actions, and you decide how to act or react in any given situation.
3. Surround yourself with other people who are working hard - To reach your goals, it is helpful to be around other people who want the same happiness and success as you. It does not matter if it is a group of peers, co-workers, or a group of like-minded friends, it's important to have people who push you to succeed.
4. Break up your tasks into smaller tasks - Think of the work you're about to do as not being so hard by breaking it down into smaller pieces of work and create small wins out of every task you create. This little pat on the back when you complete things is so motivating.
5. Stay focused - You don't always have to immediately respond to texts, emails, instant messages or even always be available. Limit your exposure to outside distractions and maybe even have a social media detox

every once in a while. Just make sure you do get back to people in a reasonable amount of time.

6. Remember your "why"- Knowing your why is the best form of motivation. The reason you are doing the work in the first place. It's crucial that you remain in touch with what inspires you.

7. Stay positive - Do what you need to do to accomplish your goals, regardless of what others might say about you. At times you will fail, but it's how you deal with failure and the lessons you learn that determines the ultimate success and happiness.

Focus on your strengths, rather than dwelling on your weaknesses. Your self-esteem will come when you develop and build on your strengths and thus keep you motivated.

Procrastination can be caused by a fear of failure, or by perfectionism. It can even come about due to a fear of success. You may subconsciously, at least fear the greater responsibilities and possibilities that may come with doing a job well. Overcoming procrastination is key to remaining focused and productive. When you procrastinate you are putting something off unnecessarily.

My biggest regret about setting up a business and running it alongside my full time day job is that I procrastinated. I spent a lot of time wondering why I wasn't doing anything. I had a plan but was not taking action or as I've heard before 'procaster planning' this indeed led me to another path of negativity and low self-worth and I needed to raise my energy levels to put myself in a happy place.

I realised on reflection that this procrastination was actually because I wasn't quite sure if the way I was running my business was right for me. I loved the idea of passive and semi passive income. However, I take my energy from others so running my business 100% online without personal in person face-to-face interactions did not match my style.

I also realised that I was scared of burning out again. As you are already aware I had to close down my award-winning 6 figure business due to burnout. I was giving to everybody else, my family, my friends, my clients, my staff, my stakeholders etc but I wasn't given to myself so I ended up giving from an empty cup and this led to me hitting rock bottom so much that I couldn't even close my business properly. I literally just walked away and spent about a year on the sofa depressed and on government benefits.

I tried to get employment but nobody would employ me, so I stopped looking. Who wanted a failed and miserable ex director or was it because I knew too much or were they wondering whether this woman was a liability. It wasn't until my mum came into my sitting room and saw me lying on the sofa in the same dressing gown for what seemed like 5 days and said there's an opportunity at the call centre at her work place and would I be interested. I basically said yes I had nothing to lose. I built back my self esteem and started to put healthy habits in place however I still looked a hot mess but I was getting there.

I realised that if I was to be truly happy and move the needle forward in my business I needed to make the most out of my time, productivity, and personal effectiveness to ensure I could spend meaningful time with those I love.

Fast forward a few years and my 'Go Happy Yourself' journey started. I retrained as a stylist and loved it however I started to procrastinate again. This time due to styling not fulfilling a motivational need. It was not until I identified that my additional business experience, modelling, career coaching and creative production was what made me unique. I could use them to support clients more effectively and that was when I was really able to find happiness in my business and the healthy habits to keep me sustained at a high energy level and motivated in my business.

You must stop procrastinating to gain happiness. I mean, I have not met or spoken to one person that has been happy about procrastinating. So, I want you to:

- Stop being a perfectionist – Spending 50% more time to improve your work by 10% probably isn't worth it. Do the best you can in the time you have, you can improve things later.
- Reward yourself for meeting goals that will link positive feelings with tasks you previously disliked.
- Breaking bigger tasks into smaller ones, with milestones, reduces the chances of feeling overwhelmed by the 'bigger picture' of a large project.
- Choose the right time of day for you and schedule tasks that require a high level of focus when you have your highest energy levels.

TASK:

Step 1: In your journal, detail any situations that cause you to procrastinate.

Step 2: Now I want you to ask yourself, what are the benefits to procrastinating and what practical, motivational tactics can you use to overcome this.

Step 3: Now, how are you going to reframe this and build new habits or do you need to do a little skills audit on yourself to identify what you could be doing to keep yourself happy?

41 / PRODUCTIVITY AND
TIME MANAGEMENT

Now let's be honest, how much time do you spend:

- Surfing the net and on social media convincing yourself that you are "working"?
- Making and accepting meaningless phone calls and having conversations that go on for far longer?
- Working on things that do not contribute to your life goals, happiness or are out of your control?
- Complaining that you have no energy or all the bad cards you have been dealt in life?
- Deciding what to focus on and chopping and changing your ideas.?
- Saying 'I'll get round to that"?

It's time to put an end to this!

You can make a huge difference to your success, energy levels, and personal satisfaction by introducing new thoughts, habits, routines, and rituals into your life. For any true success and happiness you are going to need to work on the inside and free up your attention and raise your energy levels in order to be focused and productive. So now you have had a good intro to pillar three of the 'Go Happy Yourself' journey, we are going to dig a little deeper to pave the way for the rest of your journey once you close the pages of this book. The first thing we are going to do is go back to our mindset with a few exercises.

CLEARING YOUR MIND OF CLUTTER

The first exercise I want you to do is to clear out your mental clutter. If your mind is cluttered, you will be unable to focus and work efficiently, and this is where you will flit from task to task and by the end of the day achieve nothing.

TASK:

- If you have not written down what stresses you out already, write down everything you worry about that pops into your head, day-to-day.
- Go through the list and circle everything that is outside your control and put a star next to everything that is in your control.
- Go through the list with circles, it doesn't serve you to be worrying about things you can't control, and this is a huge waste of energy. So I want you to take 3 deep breaths and as you release your breath, slowly let all these stresses go. Feel the weight lifted off your shoulders and release it to the universe. Give them love

and let them go... or maybe just kick them to the curb. It's up to you.

- Take the list of things with stars next to them and put them in priority order. You should aim for around 5-7 ideally, 10 maximum. These are the things you need to focus on as a priority.

GETTING CLOSURE AND COMPLETING THE INCOMPLETE

The emotional cost of having things that are loose ends and incomplete in our lives is a huge burden. This may be a fight with someone a year ago or money you are owed and are chasing. For these sorts of situations, you need closure.

TASK:

- Make a list of areas in your life where you need closure. Where you didn't finish something, or some business and it bothers you.
- Go through this list and the one you created earlier and prioritise the areas that bother you the most and rob you of the most energy.
- Now, either complete them or let them go. We will be going through decision making and problem solving later. If it is an emotion that you need to let go of, it is often harder to do this and you may need to address them with professional support. You should have 3-5 that you could deal with now, so go take some action on them.

BLURRED LINES OF BEING IN THE GREY ZONE.

We can all mix up what we are doing and don't enjoy or focus on one thing at a time. With so much distraction and noise, both on and offline, our attention spans are getting shorter. For example, you are with your family but are thinking about work and not being present or the other way round. This is called the grey zone.

TASK:

- Make a list of things you do when you are in the grey zone, not being present and fully focused.
- Put a star next to the things that are important to you, that need a lot of focus to be in alignment with your goals and happiness.
- Notice when you start to blur the lines, refocus yourself and be present.

ERADICATE ENERGY ROBBERS

Our body is a machine that needs food and servicing to keep us going, just like a car needs oil, an energy source, and a service to keep running at its best. If you don't take care of yourself, you will slow down and not work at your full potential. Most of us have things in our life which will be robbing us of energy. Energy robbers could be an untidy house or bad habits that you are procrastinating about changing.

TASK:

- Make a list of what is robbing you of your energy.
- Take the list and prioritise 5 things that you will take action on.

SETTING UP YOUR DAY FOR HAPPINESS AND SUCCESS

Our most powerful personal energy is our willpower, however most of us waste it by multi-tasking and resisting change. You see, most humans are quite lazy. It is our goals, routines and habits that will get us to where we want to be. Athletes and performers are perfect examples of this. When they are training towards a goal, they look very different! They have a set regime to get them to where they want to be. In order to create these habits and become more productive, we need to feel good about ourselves.

Most of our actions are unconscious but, when we have both willpower and self-awareness, we can start creating repetition and forming such an important factor for success and happiness. These are healthy habits. The exercises we have carried out should have prepared you with an awareness of yourself, your willpower will set you up to create and achieve these.

TASK:

Write down your current morning routine for the first hour and see where it needs altering to set you up right for the day.

Should you struggle with this, why not take part in the Lifestyle Challenge and download the 10 steps to a healthy, happier you PDF or take part in the Lifestyle Challenge. Both of which are available in the resource area that comes along with this book. You can find it at www.yvonnephillip.com/book

FOCUS WITHOUT FRICTION

There is a part of us that's trying to prevent our success. We have spoken about this before, your inner imposter, your limiting beliefs, imposter syndrome, comparing ourselves to others and procrastination are the main enemies of our success and happiness. As mentioned before, they are only trying to keep you safe in your comfort zone and as we already know, all growth and happiness happens outside of comfort zones.

You see our brain has three areas: the physical, emotional and conceptual. Throughout our lives, businesses, and careers we are being pulled between each part of the brain, which causes friction and inner conflict, which reduces your willpower. This leads to us giving up. To overcome this, your brain parts all need to be working as a team. This will enable you to improve your willpower and create new habits that are hardwired and become natural behaviours to us in time. Research states it takes 21 – 60 days to create a new habit but first we need to see if we can make the parts of your brain work together and in harmony so that you can get the happiness you want without conflict.

TASK:

- Close your eyes and have a conversation with yourself - why are you preventing your success and happiness? Be honest with yourself and write this down in your journal.
- Ask yourself if you seriously want to achieve, what needs to happen for you to gain the success and happiness you want.
- Now listen to your thoughts from both points of view. Try to come to an understanding of each side's motivations and see how they can work together to create the success and happiness you want.

THE PYRAMID OF PRODUCTIVITY / TASK TRIANGLE

Most of us think that writing a 'to do list' is productive, however most of the time the list is full of low value work that is not going to get us the results we really want thus is pointless.

Here is a great way to prioritise the highest value tasks, which are the most valuable activities that will get you better results. It is so important for you to identify the very highest value activities so that we do what really matters for our ideal future and happiness.

TASK:

In your journal, draw a pyramid/ triangle with 3 layers. In each layer write the following:

- The bottom layer is zero value or low pound per hour activities. These activities add very little value to your life or happiness and can be detrimental. E.g. eating junk food, smoking, drinking, gossiping, scrolling social media aimlessly.
- The second layer is high pound per hour activities. These can be marketing, selling, branding, job search, taking on that extra project at work to get the promotion.
- The third layer is high lifetime value activities that get you closer to your main goals. These can be things like starting a new health regime, starting a new business, studying, or learning.

Write 3-5 activities you do in each layer of your pyramid. You will start to notice where you are wasting your time in the bottom area. From now on, focus most of your time - at least 4 hours a day - in the top areas of your triangle and become aware of when you are not. This exercise should really make you think about what you would most benefit from spending your time on.

PRODUCTIVE ALIGNMENT

Once you have written out your pyramid of productivity, draw two circles next to each other.

Write down in one circle all of the highest value activities you know you need to focus on after you have gone through your productivity pyramid. In the other circle write all of your strengths and passions and what you enjoy spending time on personally and professionally.

The key here is that the two circles need to align, if not, you will be unhappy or not as happy as you could be as you are not doing things that you enjoy! Success without fulfilment is worthless. If it is something that you have to do but hate, try to work out a way that you can do it. For example, I hate going to the gym. However, I totally understand and appreciate that I need to stay fit and healthy if I am going to sustain myself. To bring my circles into alignment, I work out from home with different YouTubers as my PT and yoga instructors. I also have a late afternoon dance break around my studio or kitchen to get a quick cardio workout in and raise my energy levels.

Another example of productivity alignment is when I set up and grew my social enterprise to a 6 figure award winning business. However the process started with me being unemployed and sat on my bed wondering what I was going to do with myself. I was in my late 20's and had handed in my notice as a course, conference and event's organiser. I was totally unmotivated as I have been for 5, yes you heard me 5 job promotions within an organisation and was successful at securing none. The worse thing was it was not because I was not good at my job, my boss loved me but the powers at be would not promote me! This led me to being signed off work with anxiety and during this time I took a good look at myself. My strength and passion and when in my life I have been truly happy.

I came up with a list that included; dancing, modelling, the arts, business development training, organising events, community activism and creative production. I was talented at it all but did not want to retrain as an actor or dancer and did not want to be a full time model. What career would merge my strengths and passions together? I needed to find that sweet spot to reignite my happiness.

I sat down one day flicking through the local newspaper and I came across a full page advert for the Millennium Dome 2000 (now the 02 Arena Greenwich, London). They were looking for people under the age of 30 to train in Technical Theatre. Which included stage management, costume, lighting and sound etc. This opportunity was in perfect alignment for me and would mean I could be trained and possibly get a job as 5 of the lucky trainees would get a one year contract for the year 2000.

I attended the interview, secured the traineeship and then went on to get a job as a Stage Manager. I was working on a project that brought every local authority to the Dome to share the story of their town via a performance and exhibition. Through this I identify not only how powerful the arts was at addressing issues but also how powerful it had been for me as a child to express myself and have a creative outlet as one of the only black children growing up in a London overspill town in Hampshire.

Half way through the year I was promoted from Stage Manager to Project Coordinator and before my contract came to an end I started thinking about my next move and my social enterprise was born. Why because I spent my time productively, retraining, developing, networking and creating plans and taking action on what was aligned to me.

FLEXING YOUR FOCUS MUSCLE WITH THE 60-60-30 SOLUTION

The two sides of focus are quality and quantity:

- How focused are you and how long can you focus for without being distracted?
- How many different things do you work on during a day?
- How long can you focus to get good results and it is productive?
- Do you feel focused in your life strategically or are you all over the place?
- Are you doing the most important things and focused on your highest rewarding activities?

The 60-60-30 solution is a way to manage your time and focus on work for maximum results and to feel the best, energised, and on purpose.

The average person's natural productivity and focus cycle is 90-120 minutes followed by a down period of 20-30 minute. When our energy falls, we often try to power through it by eating sugary things or drinking caffeine. This is good for a short time, but we soon have a slump or crash feeling worse for it. Instead of doing this we should relax, go for a walk, meditate, lay down, do anything other than work, until our energy and focus comes back.

We will burn out if we continue not to follow the natural cycle and flow of our body. It is totally normal to feel tired after 90 minutes. You are not alone! I remember when I was in the office full time, I always needed to take a walk around 11am and 3pm. I may have taken another breaks, to grab a cuppa or pop to the loo, but I always needed that 11am & 3pm bit of fresh air. Make breaks a high priority and high quality by unplugging and relaxing, totally away from what you were doing. That way when you come back you will do better quality work with more focus.

Work in 2 blocks of one hour, then take a 30-minute break. Between the one-hour blocks take a 5-minute quick break e.g. go to the loo, grab a drink or health snack. In 30 minutes, eat then relax.   If you start to do this, you will feel more accomplished, and the great news is that you will be able to work less hours in the day but achieve more.

REFLECTION

Summarise in your journal what you need to do to be more productive moving forward

The key to having a more successful and happier life is to set boundaries that support your vision, goals, and the way you want to function. Boundaries create structure so that everyone gets the outcome they want or are at least satisfied with the outcome.

The first set is to know what you want and what you don't want. Sometimes this means saying no. Saying no can be liberating but ultimately, it brings us back to being true to ourselves.

If you find yourself feeling more overwhelmed, taking on too much, and out of balance, you need to set boundaries that support your vision and goals. If it is not working for you, say no!

If you struggle with saying no because you think it's rude or people find you aggressive, finding an assertive response is key. This will ensure you do not end up doing things you resent and that drain you. Try the following:

- "Can we look at this later in the (week, month). I am really busy right now."

- "I'd love to but if I did, I would be letting others down and I like to keep to my promises."
- "I am sorry but I have a lot on at the moment. Do you think (insert another name) would be able to help?"

Assertiveness is a behavioural philosophy and thinking style that enables people to stand up for their rights in a way that doesn't violate the rights of others. It sits between passive and aggressive behaviour. It doesn't have to be used in every encounter you have with others but behaving assertively can train others how to treat you and also get you respect amongst your family, co-workers, staff, and management.

Assertive people will not neglect their own rights, or the rights of others. They show mutual respect for the rights of all and practice assertive behaviour on a daily basis, based upon the:

- Right to make requests.
- Right to say "no" without over justification or feeling guilt.
- Right to say "yes" without feeling selfish.
- Right to be listened to, and to express your views and feelings.
- Right to take responsibility and accept the consequences for your own actions.
- Right to admit you don't understand without having to apologise.
- Right to ask for time before making a decision.
- Right to decline responsibility for the personal issues of others and withhold opinion.
- Right to judge your own worth without having to depend on the approval of others.

To become more assertive, you need to find coping and conditioning techniques that encourage you to take ownership of your own behaviour – because *'You cannot control what happens to you, but you can control what it means to you.'* (Tony Robbins).

If you have not worked out your copying and conditioning techniques, you can get stressed. As mentioned, stress is the body's physiological reaction to a perceived threat: it produces cortisol and adrenaline to increase our blood rate and breathing so that we can spring into action. This may be great for getting us out of harm's way, but not great for constructive decision making or happiness.

Let's take a look at how you can respond to others so the situation is left with an 'I'm OK you're OK' feeling for all involved.

GIVING ASSERTIVE FEEDBACK

1. Describe the issue and undesirable behaviour e.g. "When you make sarcastic remarks regarding my comments during team meetings..."
2. Define the impact e.g. "It has a negative effect and makes me feel undermined..."
3. Propose the required changes e.g. "In future, if you don't agree with my comments, please use constructive criticism opposed to sarcastic remarks..."
4. Explain the consequence of...

   a.) Changing (positive perspective): e.g. "I will feel more positive and we will get along if you change your approach..."

b.) Not changing (negative perspective): e.g. "I will inform the manager if you continue to undermine me..."

DISCREPANCY ASSERTION

Discrepancy assertion is used to point out differences between previous actions agreed and what is currently happening.

1. Previous actions agreed... e.g. "You initially mentioned the reason why the report could not be finished was due to a lack of cooperation from the sales department..."
2. Current / new proposals... e.g. "Now you are saying the report could not be finished due to a lack of training..."
3. Confirmation of priority... e.g. "Please could you confirm the reason why the report was not finished?"

DISAGREEING ASSERTIVELY

Disagreeing assertively provides options for challenging and suggesting alternative ideas.

Option A: Disagree and propose an alternative e.g. "I don't think London is the best location to hold the conference as it's not central enough for our staff in the north region. What about Birmingham?"

Option B: Disagree and ask the person to propose an alternative e.g. "I don't think London is the best location to hold the conference as it's not central enough for our staff in the north region. Can you suggest a more central location?"

Option C: Tell the person what you do agree with e.g. "I agree that the awards need to be held in a city with excellent transport links, however I am unsure that London is located central enough for our staff in the north."

MAKING REQUESTS AND REFUSING ASSERTIVELY

Persuasively making requests using the 'Broken Record Technique';

- Making direct requests. Using "I" statements to communicate needs / feelings and giving praise and facts - "I would like you to start this report after lunch please." "I am very pleased with your work."
- Showing understanding for the needs and feelings of others, whilst stating your own - "I appreciate you have a heavy workload; however, I would like you to prioritise and complete this report."
- Gaining commitment / clarifying timescales. "When do you think the report will be completed?
- Presenting the consequences of people's behaviours and actions. A last resort that must be followed through if behaviours or actions aren't changed. "If you don't complete the report, you will be put on a performance management plan. I'd prefer not to." "If you continue to undermine my comments, I will have to inform the Line Manager. I'd prefer not to."

TASK:

Go back to your list of things that stress you out. You know the ones you wrote down in pillar one of your 'Go Happy Yourself' journey and continued more recently at the start of pillar three. If you have not worked through them as yet, we need to work out a different way to deal with these situations especially if they are something you feel is out of your control and you cannot let them go. Detail in your journal how you will deal with these in an assertive way moving forward?

Delegation is an effective time management tool that can also aid your productivity. It involves making a quick decision on if you should do a task or give it to someone else. I love the 4 Ds framework. It can be used in all areas of your work, life, or business.

- Do - Work on the task as it is only small and will not take long i.e. a call, printing a report, do the dishes, load the washing machine etc
- Defer / Delay - If a task does not need to be done right away, schedule it for when you have availability i.e. a request from someone else, a report or new project.
- Delete/Drop - Remove unnecessary tasks from your schedule and move on i.e: unproductive meetings or emails.
- Delegate - Give the task to someone else.

Delegation is a 2-way process, it should not be used just to get rid of the things you don't want to do. It saves you time, develops and motivates others and grows your business and family.

However, poor delegation will cause you frustration, it demotivates and confuses others if not done correctly.

For your business and life happiness to grow and thrive you need to be able to train and develop others to take on tasks. When deciding what to delegate use the simple SMARTER framework with the E and R standing for Ethical and Recordable. There are 9 steps to successful delegation:

Step 1. Confirm to yourself that a task is suitable to be delegated and meets the criteria and framework for delegating.

Step 2. Choose the individual or team and the reasons for delegating to them that benefit both of you.

Step 3. Assess their ability and deliver any training needs they may have before handing over the task.

Step 4. Explain to the person or team why the job or responsibility is being delegated to them to ensure there are no ill feelings.

Step 5. Explain what must be done and make sure they fully understand this and how you will measure the success of the project.

Step 6. Discuss and confirm the resources, activities and services required to include the people, location, premises, equipment, money, materials and other related resources, activities and services required.

Step 7. Agree the deadline and/or review date. Make sure you double check for understanding to ensure they are not being interpreted differently.

Step 8. If you have others in your life, work, or business, make sure they know that the task has been delegated.

Step 9. It is important to also agree with the level of authority you both feel comfortable being given. Make sure you check in with the person you are working with or have delegated a task to, in order to make sure they know how they are doing and their achievements.

TASK:

Produce a list of tasks that you could delegate to free up some-time. Who will you delegate these tasks to? Start the process.

44 / EFFECTIVE PROBLEM SOLVING AND DECISION MAKING

Effective problem solving is key to success in your life, business, and career! This process of making decisions and solving problems are relatively the same!

Being successful and happy doesn't mean that you do not have any problems. It means you know how to solve them effectively as they come up. During these times, it's the ability to "think on your feet" and solve problems that counts. This decision(s) can be the difference between recovering from a crisis or not and can be taken in 7 effective steps:

Step 1: Identify the Problem

You must be clear on when there is a problem and be able to identify it. What are things like when they are the way we want them to be and how much variation are you ok with?

Step 2: Analyse the Problem

Identify the urgency of the problem. Is it at the emerging, mature or crisis stage causing real damage in terms of health, reputation, finances, etc. Are there any long-term effects?

Step 3: Describe the Problem

Create a statement of the problem that everyone involved can agree on. That way you know everyone is working toward the same goal and can come up with all the best possible.

Step 4: Look for Root Causes

This step involves asking and answering a lot of questions like:

- What caused this problem?
- Who is responsible for this problem?
- When did this problem first emerge?
- Why did this happen?
- How did this variance from the standard come to be?
- Where does it hurt us the most?
- How do we go about resolving this problem?
- Can we solve this problem for good so it will never occur again?

Step 5: Develop Alternate Solutions

Just about any problem you have to deal with has more than one solution, so it is best to develop a list of alternate solutions and decide which one will be the best for the particular problem you are facing. If you are working with a team, make sure you use the consensus to come up with the top two or three solutions that everyone involved is happy with.

Rank your possible solutions based on:

- Efficiency
- Cost
- Long-term value

- What resources you have and are able to use.

With this information you can look at the possible solutions carefully and decide what you believe to be the best solution to this problem at the time.

Step 6: Implement the Solution

Create a plan and timeline for implementing the solution, who is responsible for each element and what to do if something goes wrong. This ensures that everyone knows and understands their role and it is kept on track.

Step 7: Measure the Results

From your implementation, make sure you track and measure the results by answering questions such as:

1. Did it work? If not, go back to step 1
2. Was this a good solution?
3. Did we learn something here that we could apply to other potential problems?

As you practice this process and develop the skills, these steps will become more natural to you until the point that you are using them without noticing!

REFLECTION

What problems do you currently have that you can solve by using the 7 step problem solving scheme.

45 / GROW AND SUSTAIN YOUR SUSTAINABILITY IN ACTION

Katherine-Ann Byam Sustainable Business Strategist, Career Coach, and client. I sat down with her to discuss sustainable action for our individual happiness, the global environment, fashion, food and money.

Yvonne

I am here with my good friend and fellow business colleague Katherine Ann Byam, and she is a sustainability consultant and career coach. Thank you so much Katherine, for agreeing to be part of my book. We are going to be talking about sustainability, because that's something that's close to both our hearts in a business sense, but also a personal sense, in the way that we live our lives. So just tell people a little bit about your background, and how you got to be so passionate about sustainability.

Katherine

Oh, first of all, thanks so much, you for inviting me. It's a pleasure to be on this journey with you and to see you grow as a business professional as well.

I have a very mixed background. I came to the sustainability space from a place of wanting to do something about what I'd seen. I travelled a great deal in my last job, where I had to perform internal audits for a multinational organisation. This allowed me to see things that I would never have seen as a young woman coming from Trinidad and Tobago. The world was not just the sort of American dream that I had grown up seeing on TV. I started to recognise the biggest topic for me is the issue of inequality, and decent work.

These were the things that steered me to try to change and create something different for my future and for the future of many people. I think that burning platform really came home to me when I did my MBA in 2015/16 - there were two courses that did it for me. I was doing a course on innovation management and one of the books that was recommended reading was this book called Jugaad Innovation (which is frugal innovation-

Jugaad is the word for frugal in Hindi). They were talking about how Indians come up with amazing, frugal solutions for huge problems. So, one example in the book was refrigeration for rural communities. They couldn't buy refrigerators so they would actually mould clay in such a way that they can just put water inside this clay box and keep meat fresher for one more day. Or that someone actually corralled a lot of the engineers in her local area to design an incubator for kids. This was a solution that costs less than $100, but if you had to import something from the West, it would cost you $1000s. So, I started to realise how complicated we made things for the sake of commerce. And that was probably the biggest fire in my belly to do something different.

Yvonne

Absolutely, I had this passion for sustainability way back in my teenage years, with regard to the damage impacts that the fashion industry was having on our environment and the people that made our clothes. But at that time, I was living out of London, and we just about had a Top Shop! We didn't have any access to the fashion industry to be able to make change. But it was just something that was in me, and I started researching. That's when I started buying second-hand, because I was saddened, disappointed, and disgusted about what I was reading. And this was me as a teenager - but obviously then you don't think that you can do anything. You know, I was just like, who am I to make change? It's only in the last five years that I realised that everything we do has an impact - every buying purchase, every decision that we make in life has an effect on other people, and sustainability. I have three strategies for success, which are strategy, style, and self-care. And I remember when we were speaking before, you said, sustainability is self-care. 100%! It's about taking care of ourselves and it's about taking care of others and the world that we live in. So, I just thought that that was absolutely beautiful.

Let's explore a little bit more about the sustainability piece, because a lot of people, when we talk about sustainability, roll their eyes! I remember when I first started thinking about sustainable lifestyle and living, I was like,

"Well, what am I going to wear? I can't wear anything, because there's loads of things that conflict with each other. It's going to be too costly, as obviously, we're paying the true cost for things- it's gonna be all too much."

What would you say is a healthy definition of sustainability? I don't know if we want to go into the 17 sustainable goals a little bit more, so people can start thinking about sustainability in a wider sense.

Katherine

Yeah, I guess sustainability ultimately is being able to carry on, as we are with the same health and the same wealth that we have today. And the only way we could carry on as we are, is to rebalance things. We are carrying on as we are, we are depleting our natural resources, we are diminishing our capacity to regenerate resources. So, sustainability is really about trying to keep in balance and in check, what we have survived on and what we have thrived on, in the world. There's so many spin-off and ancillary conversations but there are 2-3 things that I'd like to really highlight about the sustainability journey. First of all, it's not just about the environment, although the environment is huge, right?

Yvonne

We live in this environment. So, it's a lot more than just that.

Katherine

Exactly, exactly. So, the environmental tipping points are a big topic of conversation right now in scientific communities and it's starting slowly to spill over into the public domain with shows and documentaries on Netflix and Amazon, etc., that are trying to promote some of these important conversations. So definitely the climate and the tipping points are important.

But the second part of it is basic life and decency. And that's the aspect of poverty, being able to feed all the people that live on this planet in a robust way, being able to drive economic growth for people who don't have a great deal of potential of economic growth or can't see it in their futures and also being able to balance the life on our planet that feeds us i.e., plants and animals. We talk about things like biodiversity loss when we have this conversation about life on this planet.

Then the third bit is about where do we see our future? I remember when I did economics, there was a debate between guns and butter - do we invest in guns? Or do we invest in butter? This was basically a corollary for food versus things. But when you really think about it, now, the conversation is more between space, and butter. We need to explore space, we need to figure out how we can leverage other planets, but at the same time, we still need to feed this one and we still need to take care of this one because it's the only one we know we can live on. So how we balance this conversation about those having competitions now to create commercial flights into space versus real deep scientific exploration into space, and how we balance that one resource that we have to leverage sustaining the planet and furthering our interest in going further in the world.

Yvonne

How do we sustain our personal brands? What changes can we make in our lives and our businesses, and our careers, to sustain ourselves? If we start with us, we can then have a ripple effect on others, and the way that they live their lives. If sustainability is about keeping ourselves in balance, and keeping ourselves moving - and earlier on in the book, we spoke about burnout and impostor syndrome, and those things that deplete us - how do we sustain our personal brand? When we think about all these other impacts that we have on the world? What things can we do as individuals?

Katherine

I love this question because as with everything in this space, there are so many ways that you can take this and make it work for you. I think the first bit is the scary bit. We have roughly 15 years to really self-correct. And what I mean by that is that there are certain climate tipping points, where if we don't change some of our behaviours and habits, those things are going to tip into irreversible effects. So, what we really want to do is to start thinking about how we can reduce our own carbon impact on the planet. Part of that is in our choices around consumption. Now, people might feel "Why do I want to have less than I have today?" It's part of our human nature to grow and to become bigger than we are. And we can still do this, but we just have to rethink the way we grow.

So, for example, you refer to the fashion industry and clothing. I still wear synthetics, because this was something that I bought over the time of earning a big salary, going out, and buying fancy things. But I refuse to buy new clothes. So, one of the things that I do is to get someone to repair my things for me and try to give them a longer life. By doing that I'm helping smaller businesses as well. So, I'm helping micro entrepreneurs, seamstresses, who are doing things that are adding value. And that's important for me. I rarely buy something new; it really has to be a special occasion.

Yvonne

And it has to be a fashion friend for life! It has to be something that you are going to wear over and over again. I still have pieces in my wardrobe, that are made from fabrics that will damage our environment. But for me to throw them away, then they're gonna go into landfill - that is still having a damaging effect. So, let's try to make the most out of what we have, because we can still look stylish and fabulous. We don't have to be always consuming the next fashion trend.

Katherine

The other thing I would say is to look at your local community. This is another easy way you can have a positive impact. Instead of ordering from Amazon, I recommend looking for someone locally who could provide the same service, possibly at a slightly higher cost, but without this level of shipping and complexity. So at least you're keeping local people surviving, right? If you can't help your community, what kind of community are you going to live in? Don't always take the easy road. It could become an easy road, if you just invest a bit of time now to find out who you can work with.

The last bit I would say about changing your own lifestyle is the conversation around meats. The bigger the animal, the more water over its life that needs to be used in order for that animal to thrive, as well as the more land that you need, etc. So, in terms of your meat choices, I'm not going to tell anyone to stop eating meat because I still eat meat. But in terms of your meat choices, go for the small animal choices and make sure that you don't overdo it.

Yvonne

I'm loving those three tips - they are absolutely perfect.

In terms of reducing consumption, you know, we have proven that we don't need to live with as much as we have been living with. So, it's about living within comfort, and living in a way that is going to make sure that there is enough for future generations.

I shop locally wherever I can, but at the same time, I know that it's a quick, easy fix to go online, because you can have purchased something within 3-5 minutes, and it can be at your door maybe that evening or the next day - but where does that economy need to be? It is better placed in our community.

I would like to talk about volunteering, and how we can support our local community by choosing maybe a charity within our values and the values of our businesses. We all have values that are 100% non-negotiable - they run through our brands. You need to think about how those values are going to show up in your brand. For example, I'm a career coach, I'm a business coach, I'm also a stylist. That's why I call myself a Success Strategist. I volunteer for a local charity that supports unemployed women back into work with interviews, and outfits. That is 100% aligned with my brand. I know that I'm helping people get out of economic poverty and feel great about themselves. When we're talking about sustainability, there are so many different ways that you can sustain yourself and fill your cup up, as well as help other people.

Katherine

Absolutely, I think it's important to do what we can, but also, I want to acknowledge that not everybody is going to feel like they have the time to give up. So, you can give money, you can give time, you can give help and support, guidance, you can teach, you can volunteer to do lectures in schools.

Yvonne

Yes! If you've got old things - you can give them to a charity shop.

Katherine

That's a really important point. Just yesterday, I was having a conversation about minimalism and how it helps us in our mental health. It's so important for us to recognise that the stuff around us is clogging our minds. It's creating a stress that doesn't need to be there because you need to find space for all these things that you're accumulating. So why not take some of those things and give them to someone who's in need? Marie Kondo your flat, give the things away that you don't need.

Yvonne

Having a clear mind enables you to be able to focus on what you want, and your goals. If you need to clear that space, you need to do it, because that's going to enable you to show up as yourself and in a positive way. Because cluttered minds are confused minds. That then has a knock-on effect in terms of your motivation, your self-esteem.

Katherine

I got pulled up yesterday, and rightfully so, by someone who is in the neurodiversity space. It's very easy for us to say that the cluttered mind means a cluttered head, because sometimes some people process in this way. And that's something that we need to acknowledge. But I definitely believe that for me, I have too many things that I've accumulated over many years of having a salary and being in the consumer rat race. The last time I bought something new, I bought it from a sustainable place.

Yvonne

Going back to the cluttered mind meaning a cluttered head - I think that goes back to the start of the book where it's about knowing yourself and digging deep to understand who you are, how you work and how you want to show up. No matter if you have that cluttered mind or cluttered space, if that's okay with you, if that fuels you and gives you energy, then that's going to sustain you and that's going to move you forward. But if you know that it doesn't have that effect then that's something that you need to work on.

Katherine

Absolutely, I totally agree with that.

Yvonne

So, let's talk about sustaining yourself personally and what sustainable success looks like. For me, I have values around reducing waste, fair trade, and economic impact. But a lot of people will look at our sustainability goals, and think, "Wow, I can't, I can't do all of this, it's, it's too much." My advice would be to just pick a few that you're gonna go deep on and then a couple that you can go wide on whilst you're getting used to developing a new way of living and a new way of thinking. As an expert in this field, how should people start their sustainable success and what should it look like for them?

Katherine

One of the important things for service-based businesses is that we tend to take for granted the impact of digital impact. The digital impact that we have is the number of emails that we store, how heavy your websites are to load, the number of places that we show up - all of this creates a digital impact that creates an energy consumption impact, which we underestimate.

Yvonne

I'm sorry, but I have to put my hands up, I've never thought about digital impact, because you don't think that it's taking up space.

Katherine

Yeah, that's a big energy suck. So, thinking about how you design your websites, thinking about those images that you use, thinking about cleaning out the old stuff such as blog posts that you may have on there that you're not using. All of these things contribute to energy consumption that we can start revising.

The other thing I would suggest is to create more digital templates for people to use rather than asking them to print.

Another thing is this whole idea of a circular economy. So, if you are product based, in particular, it's worth your time to do the research as to how people can dispose of your item. So, giving people ideas about how to do that is very useful. If it can be recycled, tell them where it can be recycled, or how to find information about how it can be recycled in their area. If it can be repurposed, you can give them ideas about who is repurposing it and what kinds of things they're doing with the repurposed items. Then if it has to go to landfill, you can make sure that the materials you use do break down and go back to the earth in a clean way.

Yvonne

Printing is a really interesting one. When I was in the office, I was printing left, right and centre. I was still old school - I like paper! But since I've been working from home, I haven't purchased a printer, and I haven't had the need for a printer. So, it really proves that you can do without most things, and you will always find a way. There are things in our lives that we feel are essential, that really aren't essential. So just think - can I do without it? The answer will probably be yes.

Then the circular economy. There's a circular economy within style and fashion where people are now starting to rent clothing, which is a great idea on paper. However, we're still using air miles and transportation to get this item to this client. So, is it really helping? Because there's still a lot of damage that's been done to the environment.

Katherine

This is one of the reasons I really drive the whole idea of 'think local' because it becomes a non-issue. If you have a central hub in your local community then this is a great way to combat that. Another thing is clothing swaps which are becoming really popular now too. You take your stuff and start trading items and you suddenly have a whole new wardrobe! These are all great ideas.

We talk about our money stories, and these always come up in our sustainability conversations, as there is always a big conflict around money and sustainability. There is a need for us to make money as the world still runs on it but not everything needs money.

Yvonne

Yes! It was natural to do clothing swaps and have your clothes made in the past. There was always a dressmaker/seamstress in your community. You had things that were made so well, and they are unique. The 80s fast fashion boom happened and all that went out of the window, and we all became carbon copies of each other!

I love that you mentioned clothes swaps as they are my absolute favourite way of being sustainable. It's like a day out for me! It becomes part of my self-care and a way of meeting other like minded people. It's a no brainer.

I would like to talk about Greenwashing and the issues around bigger brands doing the "right thing" in terms of sustainability and ethical trade, but making things seem better that they really are. If someone wants to go along the sustainable lifestyle route, how can they watch out for the green washers?

Katherine

We need these guys to be better as they still control so much of the marketplace, so we need to hold them accountable. As they start out on their journey, they need to check what they are committing to and balance that. Now people are starting to do Environmental Social Governance reporting in the big companies. It is a new way for investment banks to challenge organisations on their ethics and their values before they fund them. A criterion for investors now is that they have considered the environment in what they are doing. This is a great pivot point. However, it also has become a trigger for some of the green-washing we have seen. They are jumping onto it because they know it has a real material impact on their lending rates, so they are jumping in and saying where they are before they have really got there.

I would also look at their underlying ethos as well. One of the things I call brands out for a lot is this whole idea of open innovation. Very recently, I saw a very famous brand announce that they had come up with some packaging that is completely clean for the environment and that they have patented it. If you have designed something that is game changing for the planet - why is it patented? Even Elon Musk opened up his battery technology for other firms. We need to check in and see what they are really doing. Yes, it is great that they are making great packaging but there is another question about how they are protecting these things that are super important to the environment. I would really encourage brands to rethink some of their IP protections.

Yvonne

Absolutely. Sustaining ourselves and the planet – it's not about profit. We need to sustain our economy, yes, and we need to make sure things are affordable, but ultimately, we need to change our money mindset when it comes to sustainability. By paying a higher price, we are going to get better quality and longevity.

Katherine

Money mindset around sustainability is a big topic and it's a topic that is going to evolve a lot as we go forward. If we were to think about it at a national level, growth still makes sense. If we think about it on a global level, growth isn't really possible. We have a finite planet, therefore there is no real growth we can have. We have to rethink what we attach to growth, value and quality of life and what that really means. Quality of life doesn't necessarily mean a swimming pool. A simple thing such as taking a hike along the coast can give you the same utility and more than some of the luxurious things.

The other side of the story is this whole idea of luxury is changing with sustainability. Sustainable things are the new luxury.

Yvonne

100%!! I was at a summit the other day and it was about living a luxury lifestyle and my version of that is buying sustainable and being at one with the planet. This is my luxury. The other guests just didn't get it as they were all about fast cars and swimming pools.

Katherine

When you start about thinking to identify an original piece, it's all about uniqueness. That pushes the perceived value up in the world. If we are still thinking on a national scale, these ideas of attaching value to things that are scarce and rare still exist. At a global level, it doesn't really make sense. We are not yet set up to operate at a global level, which is a concern, but let's start where we can start.

Yvonne

Absolutely!

In terms of where we can start, what do we want to advise to the readers if they want to build a sustainable brand, whether it be for personal use or their businesses? What would be the first thing they should start with? We have one which is knowing yourself, but what are some of the other things?

Katherine

Acknowledge what you really need versus your desires and your wants and seeing how you can replace the feeling that you want to have in your life with something that is more natural and organic (for example, that walking on the coast reference) I have just come back from Cornwall, and it was incredible - I underestimated the beauty of this country.

Look and see how you can appreciate what is around you and how you can set yourself up to take more from all your experiences. A lot of us walk through our experiences dead as we are constantly thinking about the next thing rather than being in the moment.

These are really important principles to live by.

We talk about travel, and I wouldn't be where I am today on this sustainability path without it. One of the things I am grateful for in my last job, is that when I visited a country, I would live like a local for at least 2 months. That has really changed my perspective. But for you to appreciate that, we need to rethink a lot of things in order to allow people to enjoy cultures in that way. Reading, listening to podcasts, watching films and documentaries - it's about stepping into that context and being present. It is something you can practice and grow into.

Yvonne

Most definitely. Being present and knowing yourself will allow you to start thinking about how you are going to build sustainability into your brand, so that you can keep yourself at a certain level of energy, income, whilst helping the planet or helping others. If you don't, on a personal level you are going to burnout and start feeling less than. When you are working on your mindset you also need to start thinking about how you are going to sustain yourself for the future.

Katherine

I would love to close the loop on the money mindset question. I had an opportunity to reflect on that just recently. I am of the mindset that to a certain extent, money leads to greed and greed leads to unsustainable practices. I have had a very strong model in my mum, in terms of how to approach money and the four principles that she taught me.

1. Save so you have the opportunity in the future to do more.
2. Be generous. Recognise that you need to give to the flow of money in order to get it back.

3. Think about how to generate it and be creative with ways of earning.

4. Always keep a track and remember that money is a tool to help you - yourself, and your community.

46 / MONEY AND HAPPINESS

What does money mean to you and does it bring you happiness? Some people see money as a means to an end living month to month, pay cheque to pay cheque. Others see it as the many metaphors mentioned earlier; it does grow on trees, it's the route of all evil etc. Ultimately our goal in life should be to be happy and healthy. With this in mind I see money as a means of getting what you want and need quicker and easier.

Money does not bring you happiness but it does allow you to do the things that make you happy. You must understand where and what you want to be in life and use money, obtain money and create money (legally) to bring you that. This could be through working towards a job promotion or career change. Starting a part-time or full time business that you are passionate about. Or getting more visible so that you attract more clients.

Your mindset around money has to be abundant and authentic. You have to have a positive mindset around money and this book would have hopely given you some of the self awareness and development you need to support that.

We live in a fast paced consumer age where people are always on the move. Where people are renting a flash car at the weekend to socialise and show off fake images of wealth but are travelling on the bus Monday - Friday. Bloggers are presenting themselves in designer clothing that they often take back to the stores after they have snapped that all important photo or video. A person's success is now based on his or her net worth, the value of the property they live in. We are being programmed to want more and hustle harder. Trying can be exhausting and is not sustainable on its own.

Ask yourself the question: do you need these material things and how is it contributing to your happiness? Do not feel pressure to impress others with the money you have, instead use it to create the happiness you want now.

We are told to save for the future and build a nest egg for retirement. Life is too short and what is the point is having all this money in the bank if you cannot enjoy it. Now I am not saying don't save, we need to think about our future but we also need to live in the present as tomorrow is not always guaranteed.

At the end of pillar one of this book we set your goals and the rewards you want to give yourself when you achieve them. These rewards should be based on the happiness you want in your life, career or business but you should also stretch yourself and get big goals and big rewards. Invest in different experiences that will widen your future. They will give your acceptance and validation in who you are and assist you in creating the greater happiness you want.

47 / FINAL THOUGHTS

As you come to the end of this book I wanted to leave you with some final thoughts, a little motivation and something to remember as you continue your 'Go Happy Yourself' journey'.

Happiness and success is not linear and is not a given in life. You have to create it and whilst creating it there will be highs and lows, peaks and troughs of emotions and challenges. There is no straight line to your destination. It can be a squiggly line of confusion that you need to navigate to get clarity and build your confidence.

At times you will feel exhilarated throwing your hands in the air and doing a happy dance as you reach that highpoint and celebrate a win. Feelings of joy, contentment and fulfilment will wash over you. Other times you will find out that what you thought would bring you happiness is not quite what you thought it would be.

At times like these you may start to compare your version of happiness and success to others and this could hold you back even more. This brings me to my final story.

I was just coming to the end of the pilot beta test delivery of what is now my signature program which is now called Visibility for Success. I had test driven it with five lovely ladies and I had already received some fantastic testimonials and feedback on the programme, I was on a complete high. I was preparing to launch it to the wider online world when I noticed another coach who was also a graphic designer launching a program with similar messaging to mine. This stopped me in my tracks, I didn't know what to do. She was dynamic and younger than me and had a host of design skills which I didn't.

I could only talk about design as I learned from my time in the creative industries. What was I to do? What did I do? I stopped and halted my programme's full launch completely! I went into a well of self pity and self doubt and shelved it for 3 years, 3 years of doing nothing with it. 3 years of trying different things and nothing really quite meeting the energy levels, excitement and motivation that I had when I was delivering the pilot programme.

I watched in envy as the other coach and brand designer crushed her goals and showed up as her happy self. About 2 years into my 3 year hiatus I received a call from another coach who was working with said brand design coach. They were inviting me to be their style speaker on their joint mastermind. I was totally floored that this woman didn't see me as competition, she wanted to collaborate. She could see how my skills actually added to hers. She didn't really know who I was at the time, she was just growing her business and creating her happiness based on her values, passion and beliefs.

I wasn't on her radar but due to what I was seeing online and what people were saying about her I saw myself as less than. I was comparing myself to her and not taking into account the unique qualities that I had and what I was bringing to the personal branding space. I delivered what is now my Day of Style online event and their clients absolutely loved it. Since then I've worked 1:1 with a number of the entrepreneurs that attended, styling their personal brands. She has delivered in my client support group The Success Sisterhood and we have even been on a night out to a cabaret in London becoming friends.

Why had I stopped myself? It was because I was comparing myself and letting my limiting beliefs take over. What you see and believe about others is often only half of the picture. In my case the success and happiness of the person I was comparing myself to was true and genuine but what I wasn't seeing was what was unique about me and what I have to offer.

At times like these when something knocks you off course and you are feeling less than I would invite you to refer back to this book and your journal. Remember all the work you have done on and for yourself. I want you to remember what is unique about you. I want you to remember why you started on this journey in the first place and the results you have achieved so far no matter how large or how small.

If you have done the reflections and tasks you should have had some great results whether it be the development of a strategy, the uplevel of your style or the skills to sustain your self-management. There should have been at least one milestone or light bulb moment that you can refer back to.

Your journey to happiness will take time and sometimes you will go down the wrong path. I don't want you to get hung up on this or start to compare yourself to others. That will only hinder you. What I want you to do is remember all the achievements and good feelings you have had and celebrate those wins.

Remember you are a unique, amazing, holistic human being that deserves the success and happiness you want on your terms. Don't hold yourself back or listen to the naysayers. Just stay true to you and 'Go happy yourself'

ACKNOWLEDGEMENTS

SPECIAL THANKS TO

Doreen Thompson-Addo for unknowingly starting me on my happiness journey. Cleopatrice Andrew for our frank, unfiltered conversations and your emotional support prior and during my book writing process.

My clients Rachel Power, Merrisha Gordon, Jane Edis and Katherine Ann Byam who have been the willing participants of interviews and images for this book.

Lisa Johnson for giving me this opportunity to step out of my comfort zone, write this book and share my journey and expertise to support others. And last but by no means least Abigail Horne and the team at Authors and Co for supporting me through this book writing and publishing process.

CREATIVE CREDITS TO

My amazing team for this project; Amanda Hutchinson, Aubrey Fagon, Ru Mel and Hayley Forster who have my clients and I looking absolutely fabulous in the visuals that support this book and its additional resources.

ABOUT THE AUTHOR

Yvonne (Yves) Phillip is a Holistic Success and Visibility Consultant that supports entrepreneurs and employees to elevate their brands through strategy, style and self-care.

Coined the 'The Visibility Queen' and 'Style Wing Woman' by her clients and coaches. Yves has a 30 year portfolio career that has included corporate, community and the creative sectors. Yves has worked as a Model & Dancer, Video Director/Producer, Lifestyle Magazine Writer, Speaker & Presenter, Sustainable Stylist (Personal and Fashion), Event & Stage Manager, Trainer & Project Manager, Career Coach, Ninja Networker and has set up and ran an awarding winning multi six figure social enterprise.

Setbacks and challenges have been a part of her journey, but she embraces these in her commitment to personal growth. Raising her child as a single mother while performing in a 9-5 job and running a social venture was not easy. She found ways to build the mindset and the self-care routines that averted crisis in these tough moments. Yves uses her personal transformation from broke, busted and burnout to successful, stylish and sustainable to inspire others on their personal journeys. Yves firmly believes that if you present your authentic self, have a strategy, and take action anything is possible.

Yves solutions empower you to look great on the outside, feel fabulous on the inside and have a mindset and strategy to achieve the success and balance you deserve out of your life, business and career. She offers products, services, training and events to support your personal branding, business growth and style transformation.

Yves is a Londoner with Caribbean roots. She champions diversity and inclusion, sustainability and fairtrade and also finds the time to volunteer with the employment charity Smart Works. Her other favourite things are "Mum time" spa days, ice cream, basketball and a late afternoon dance break.

If after reading this book you need a little more support you can work with Yves in various different ways and levels.

1:1 SUPPORT

- Power hour – Ideal if you have a specific topic or activity that you need support with. Yves can work wonders in just one hour.
- Strategy Day – Spend a half or full day with Yves to work out what is right for you and produce your personalised action plan.
- Accountability – Ideal for ongoing support with your success and visibility strategy, style and selfcare

ONLINE COURSES

- Style For Success – An online course with access to my private group The Success Sisterhood and coaching call that will answer all your questions and take you style to the next level.

- Self - Management for Success – An online course with access to my private group The Success Sisterhood that will ensure you sustain your success with self-management techniques and coaching calls.
- Visibility for Success - An online course with access to my private group The Success Sisterhood that will take your personal brand to the next level.

IN PERSON EXPERIENCES

- Seasonal Style Shoot – A group day that includes all you need to get your brand to the next level through with photo or video. Includes a 1:1 with Yves with hair and makeup optional.
- Sustainable Style Seminar and Shopping – A fun day or half day around the city learning, shopping and styling yourself in a sustainable ways.
- Success with Soul Visibility Retreat – A 3–5 day retreat in a relaxed but productive group setting to consolidate your visibility strategy and build you branding assets to include photos, videos, social media & PR.

CORPORATE

Yvonne is also available to speak at corporate events and to deliver training to support and develop your staff to grow within the workplace. Create a more diverse and equal environment and thought leaders for the future through women's leadership, women's wellbeing and female inclusion.

For more Information on 1:1 services, programmes and in person experiences, visit www.yvonnephillip.com

YouTube:
https://www.youtube.com/channel/
UCM1lJYfbJ1ASGzNAviZrwLw

📘 facebook.com/YvonnePhillipTheSuccessStylist

📷 instagram.com/yvonnephillipthesuccessstylist

💼 linkedin.com/in/yvonnephillip

📌 pinterest.com/YvonnePhillipTheSuccessStylist

Printed in Great Britain
by Amazon

83659772R00171